DOUBLE PLAY

DOUBLE PLAY
FAITH AND FAMILY FIRST

BEN & JULIANNA
ZOBRIST

WITH MIKE YORKEY

B&H
PUBLISHING GROUP
NASHVILLE, TENNESSEE

978-1-4336-8331-2

Published by B&H Publishing Group
Nashville, Tennessee

Dewey Decimal Classification: B
Subject Heading: ZOBRIST, BEN \ BASEBALL PLAYER—
BIOGRAPHY \ CHRISTIAN LIFE

1 2 3 4 5 6 7 8 • 18 17 16 15 14

This book is dedicated to Zion and Kruse, God's gifts to us through our love for each other. We wanted you to have these stories in detail so that you would know how God has orchestrated the love between us. It is never perfect, and often difficult, but we enjoy the story God has given us to proclaim His grace in our lives. He truly holds all things together (Col. 1:17).

ACKNOWLEDGMENTS

This book has taken some serious teamwork to come into fruition. Many, many thanks to Mike Yorkey, Dawn Woods, Dave Schroeder, and Jay Schield for your creativity, your love for our family, and your dedication to excellent work. Much love from the Zobrist fam.

CONTENTS

INTRODUCTION

BEN

Nearly three hundred times a year, I leave the on-deck circle and approach home plate at Tropicana Field, the domed stadium that's home to my team, the Tampa Bay Rays.

My gait is slow and purposeful as I carry a 34-inch, 32-ounce F165 Louisville Slugger, weighted and balanced to my specifications. Toward the top of the flame-tempered bat, my name is etched into the wood. For a kid who grew up playing backyard Wiffle ball games in a small Illinois farm town, that's pretty cool.

During the five seconds or so that it takes me to reach the batter's box, a song plays loudly on the huge speakers suspended from the rafters. Every home team batter who comes to the plate gets to choose a "walk-up" song that plays in the background.

I know my walk-up song well because I know the singer even better. Every time I step up to the plate, I hear the soaring, angelic melodies of my wife, Julianna. Out of the 750 major league baseball players, I'm sure that I'm the only batsman who takes the plate with his better half singing in the background.

That's pretty cool too.

I've been using Julianna's songs as my walk-up music since the 2009 season. I got some good-natured teasing in the clubhouse for bringing my wife onto the field, so to speak. "Is that a girl singing?" one of my teammates asked. The typical walk-up song has a big bass-driven beat, a manly kind of feel with growly vocals. Think heavy metal or hip-hop. Julianna's music has a beat but with more of a rock pop sound.

"Yeah, that's Julianna," I said. "Isn't she great?"

Just as it's my desire to use my God-given talent on the baseball field, I want Julianna to use her God-given gift for music to impact others.

One of the first songs she wrote, "The Tree," was my walk-up music for the 2009 and 2010 seasons, followed by "Only You" in 2011 where Juliana sang, *I want you and only you and no one else will ever do*. She wasn't singing about me but rather our Lord and Savior. In 2012 and 2013, I chose "Behind Me." (Sample lyric: *I'm going crazy/trying to find my way again/gotta leave it all behind me . . .*)

Singing is something my artistic-minded wife loves to do, just as I love playing baseball. She's been singing in public since junior high when she joined the worship band at her father's church.

I like being in a supporting role for Julianna's musical aspirations, which is why we live near Music City—Nashville, Tennessee—during baseball's offseason. Nobody recognizes me on Music Row or in downtown Franklin, our hometown, which is fine by me. If folks do, they leave us alone. That's quite a contrast to Tampa Bay, where things can get pretty intense during the baseball season.

Julianna and I have been married eight years, and we're a close-knit couple. I admire how Jules—as her close friends and I call her—puts herself out there, baring her soul and her artistic side on stage. She has a passion for performing as well as letting her creative juices flow when she gets into a recording studio with a producer.

How God brought together two pastors' kids from the nation's heartland to form a double-play combination, if you will, is a unique story that we love to share. We both come from large families: Julianna grew up with five siblings in Iowa City, Iowa, and I come from a family of five children that planted roots in the checkerboard farmlands of Eureka in central Illinois.

Now we're teaming up in *Double Play*. As you'll soon read, there were too many coincidences and "God things" that happened along the way not to believe that the Lord brought us together as part of His plan for our lives.

JULIANNA

My husband is the greatest, and he'll do anything to support me, as our story will illustrate.

A couple of years ago, I was in my snowy hometown of Iowa City, Iowa, visiting my parents with Ben, and our two children, Zion and Kruse. The month was January, and we were a month away from the start of baseball's spring training. Ben was preparing for his seventh year playing for the Tampa Bay Rays.

Whenever we're in my hometown, my dad—Jeff Gilmore, the pastor of Parkview Church—often invites me to lead the singing with the worship band. Ever since I've been a little girl, I've loved to perform in front of others, especially when I can sing about God's love and glorious nature.

On this particular Sunday morning, before the first of three services, I stepped off the stage and found a quiet place to be by myself. I always have this private moment, especially in a church, so that I can pray and ask the Lord for wisdom on how I should sing that day. If I am not familiar with the church, I don't want to perform in such a way that people are uncomfortable. At the same time, I like to be . . . energetic and exuberant. It's all about finding the right balance sometimes. My main goal is to share the message of Christ in an entertaining and compelling way, so if the way I perform—or even dress—hinders that goal, then I want to be careful.

I prayed, and I felt like the Lord was directing me to perform like I always do. In other words, have fun doing it. Throw caution to the wind.

I went out there and sang my heart out. I had a blast leading Dad's congregation through singing worship songs. Even though I was pretty spent after the third service, my energy was revived when an excited woman sought me out afterward.

"You're *such* a wonderful singer and fantastic performer," she exclaimed. "I'm a producer with the MovieGuide awards show that takes place in Los Angeles in two weeks, and we just had an artist cancel on us. Would you be interested in singing in her place?"

My heart sank. "We're going to be in Dallas," I replied. "My husband is committed to speaking at a baseball banquet at his old school, Dallas Baptist University. I'm supposed to be there."

"Oh, that's too bad, but I understand. It's short notice and everything. Maybe next time . . ."

"Wait a minute," I said. "Let me talk to Ben. Maybe something could be worked out."

When I told Ben about the opportunity, he didn't blink an eye. "Yeah, you need to do this. It'll be a great experience." He was just as thrilled as me that I'd get to sing in front of a star-studded audience on national TV.

The logistics of going out to the West Coast for an awards show were a bit difficult, but what we worked out was that our three-year-old son, Zion, would stay with Ben in Dallas, where my sister Liz and her family lived. Then my mother, Cheryl Gilmore, and I would fly from Dallas to Los Angeles with my five-month-old daughter, Kruse, on my lap. The welcome news that the MovieGuide folks would provide first-class tickets was another indicator that this was a big deal.

The 2012 MovieGuide Faith & Values Awards Gala was a special evening where a full house of Christian movie stars, producers, and executives would gather to honor movies and television programs that inspire viewers rather than offend them. The annual event is known as the "Christian Oscars" in the entertainment industry.

For someone who had grown up in the Midwest, I felt like I was in a movie when I arrived at the Universal Hilton Hotel near the heart of Hollywood. Black limos stretched for more than a block. Glamorous actresses stepped out in shimmery dresses from Christian Dior and Oscar de la Renta, on the arms of handsome men in double-breasted tuxedos. A scrum of cameramen jostled for position and called out to stars like Corbin Bernsen of *L.A. Law*, James Patrick Stuart of *Call of Duty*, and Dean Cain, the emcee for the evening who starred in *Lois & Clark: The New Adventures of Superman* and *Beverly Hills 90210*, the drama series that aired in the 1990s. I thought I recognized a few singers from the current season of *American Idol*.

This was my first red carpet experience! I love fashion and dressing up, so before I went to Los Angeles, I shopped for a stylish new outfit. I was in seventh heaven clicking through the Saks Fifth Avenue website and finally chose a black sleeveless evening dress with sewn-on silver sequins in a zebra pattern. The knee-length outfit from Torn by Ronny Kobo lifted my confidence because I had delivered a baby five months earlier and wanted to look my best. I also had my hair stylist back home in Franklin streak several tresses of my long black hair in three shades of vibrant color: fuchsia, "My Little Pony" pink, and Derby Clementine, which was a tangerine-colored hue.

Even though I didn't have a gorgeous guy in black tie escorting me, I still had a great time walking the red carpet with a MovieGuide-logoed backdrop. I understood where I was on the food chain and knew the cameras weren't necessarily pointed in my direction, but it was fun pretending that the paparazzi were yelling, "Look this way, luv" at me.

Actually, several camera crews were interested in interviewing me, including Cooper Harris with Media Mingle TV. She was chatty and spirited, in keeping with the energy of the event.

"I'm here with Julianna Zobrist, who not only has amazing style but also amazing talent," Cooper began in the form of an introduction. "She will be performing later this evening."

"I am! I'm singing 'Say It Now,' a new song off my EP coming out April 10." My smile had to be over one hundred watts.

"That's so exciting!" Cooper gushed. "Is this your first album?"

"It's my second, but it's my first real push."

"What is the gist of your music? What is your genre?"

"My genre? I don't really know if you can categorize me. Pop, fun, dancey. It's Christian pop, basically."

I noticed Cooper looking at my multicolored hair. "I think your hair is gorgeous," she said. "I love it. It's kind of inspirational. But I have to ask you about your husband. I'm a huge, huge geek when it comes to baseball players. What's he like?" she asked conspiratorially.

I was used to questions like this. "He's *totally* normal! He's amazing and the best man in the world in my opinion."

"He plays for the Rays, right?"

Cooper knew her ballplayers, but I figured many viewers would have no idea who the Rays were. "Yes, he plays for the Tampa Bay Rays. He's their second baseman," I said.

When the two-minute interview was over, a couple of other camera crews caught my attention for snappy stand-up interviews, which I was glad to do. Then I made my way backstage to prepare myself.

I was extremely nervous. Maybe it was all the cameras, all the Hollywood people, or the knowledge that the MovieGuide awards show would be broadcast nationwide on the Hallmark Channel with a potential audience in the millions, but I had plenty of butterflies bumping into each other inside of me. I'd sung in a lot of big churches, before big crowds when I was in college, but this was a big step up.

I found a quiet place backstage and started running the lyrics of "Say It Now" through my head. I had *never* done that before. I knew the song really well—I had written the lyrics—but I was nervous that I'd have one of those deer-in-the-headlights moments and freeze onstage. That's every performer's worst nightmare.

There was another concern. During rehearsal that afternoon, the show's producers were very specific about where I needed to be at certain parts of the song. For instance, at the end of the first chorus, they wanted me facing stage left, where they would have a camera ready for me. Then as I started the second verse, I was to turn to my right and start walking stage right, where cameras on *that* side of the ballroom were waiting for me.

Since I was coming on just past the midpoint of the awards show, I had time to rehearse the lyrics and mentally prepare myself—and pray. It was also tricky walking around on the steel stairs because I was in stilettos, and I didn't want my long, thin high heels to slip into the openings. Walking on my tippy toes solved that problem.

Finally, I was introduced by cohost Joe Mantegna, star of the ABC show *Criminal Minds*. The techno-beat track of "Say It Now" was piped in, and I was dialed up and ready to go. I sang smoothly as I walked toward stage left, looked into the camera, and moved into the first chorus:

> *Be more, be more than beautiful*
> *You're not, you're not some stupid girl*
> *You've got something to say so*
> *Say it now, say it now, say it now*
>
> *Be more, be more than typical*
> *It's not a make believe world*
> *You've got something to say so*
> *Say it now, say it now, say it now*

After four minutes and eighteen seconds of performing, I heard thunderous applause as I took a bow. Everything came off well, and I was extremely pleased. Talk about a big high as I walked off the stage. I could have floated back to Dallas where Ben and Zion were waiting for my return.

As I caught my breath in one of the dressing rooms, I thought about another question that Cooper Harris had asked me on the red carpet: "What's your message?"

Here's how I answered: "My message is mostly to young girls and young women, basically because I am one, so I can relate. I want young girls and women not to feel like they have to be perfect. I think there is a lot of pressure that we put on each other, for no reason than to be someone we can never be. I want girls to love who they are and love who the Lord made them to be, to embrace that and be bold." What I meant was that you can't be perfect, and that is why Christ came to this Earth.

That's where *Be more than beautiful, you're not some stupid girl* came from.

I wrote that lyric because something horrible happened to me when I was twelve years old.

LEADING OFF

BEN

I come from a baseball family.

I was always swinging a bat, throwing a ball, fielding grounders, or catching flies growing up. Since my father, Tom Zobrist, had played a lot of baseball when he was younger and loved the game, he put a neon yellow plastic bat into my grubby hands as soon as I could stand on my own two feet. He loves telling anyone who will listen that the first time I took BP—batting practice— was in our living room. I was two years old, swinging my plastic bat at a plum-sized plastic ball he underhanded from several feet away.

It didn't take long for me to get the hang of connecting the skinny bat with the gently pitched ball. I loved knocking that white orb around the living room, spraying the ball to all fields. Dad got a kick out of me connecting with his toss-ups—until the time I knocked over a lamp. That's when Mom announced that we had to move batting practice to the backyard.

We were living in Kansas City, Missouri, at the time, while Dad was attending Calvary Bible College and preparing to become a church pastor. I was the second of what would become five children and his first son. In the backyard of our modest rental, he positioned me so that I could hit for the fences—the back of the house. If I hit the Wiffle ball onto the roof, I made a home run. At age four, there was nothing more fun than hitting the plastic ball high up on the roof and watching it dribble back toward us.

A lot of the seminary students were fathers of young children, so Dad never had a problem putting a backyard game together. He'd be the pitcher for both teams—and the umpire—keeping the game organized and moving along. In the summer, we never wanted to go in for dinner and begged him for one more at-bat.

I played other sports besides baseball growing up. I liked kicking goals on the soccer field, shooting baskets in the driveway, and catching long passes in touch football. Even if I was playing pick-up games with my friends, I loved competition and always had to win, which got me into trouble one time . . .

We had moved to Eureka, Illinois, population 5,000, the summer before I started first grade. That year, I can remember waiting for the lunch bell to ring at Davenport Elementary School. In less than a minute, we were expected to line up alphabetically and slowly walk to the boys' and girls' bathrooms, where we would wash our hands before we could go to the cafeteria for lunch. With a last name like Zobrist, I was always last, although there were times when they reversed things and I got to be first in line.

On this particular day, I had to line up last after the lunch bell rang. The girl in front of me, Mandy Yoder, wasn't keeping up as we inched forward. Couldn't she see that we were losing ground?

I had ants in my pants. I couldn't be the last to lunch. When we got close enough to the boys' bathroom, I spotted my chance. I broke for the door, pushing my way past slowpoke Mandy. Maybe I knocked her over.

Once I got inside the restroom, I could make up ground since no teachers were around. I jostled and elbowed my way past several classmates to one of the sinks, where I quickly dabbed my hands under the faucet and wiped my hands on my shirt.

I hustled out to the hallway with several classmates. We knew not to sprint because there was a "no running" policy in school hallways. That didn't stop us from speed walking, though. I was working my arms like an Olympian when my teacher stopped me.

"Young man, I saw you knock over Mandy," Miss Leman said. "I'm giving you a referral."

I had never gotten a referral before, but it didn't sound good.

The next day, the bell rung at the end of school—and I was surprised when my parents walked into the classroom. For some reason, I knew I was in trouble.

Dad spoke first. "Ben, Miss Leman tells me that you were pushing kids so that you could beat them to the bathroom and get to the cafeteria before anyone else."

I lowered my head. I didn't know what to say. He and Mom looked really serious.

"Look, God doesn't want us to be No. 1 all the time," Dad continued. "Sometimes He wants us to follow, so what your mother and I want you to do from now on is give deference to your classmates and let them go first whenever you get the opportunity. You need to let them go ahead. You need to learn to be polite. You don't always have to be first to do something."

That was a hard lesson to learn because of my competitive nature. I *always* had to win, whether we were playing H-O-R-S-E in the driveway or rolling the dice in Monopoly. Many times, I would create a competition in my head so that I have something to shoot for—like beating my classmates to the cafeteria.

"Yes, Dad."

My days of pushing past classmates were over, but my days of playing organized baseball began the summer after first grade when Dad signed me up for a Little League team comprised of seven-, eight-, and nine-year-old ballplayers. I had a bad "baseball birthday"—May 26. The cutoff date for our league was June 1, which meant that for the rest of my Little League career, I would always be competing against older kids.

I saw this as just another form of competition. I loved the challenge of playing against bigger kids who were one, two, or close to three years older than me. I hit the ball well and even held my own when I pitched, despite the age difference. (This was player-pitch baseball, not coach-pitched.) I loved playing any position, but there was something extra about being a pitcher. I relished the opportunity to get batters out or get them to swing and miss on strike three. There was something about the one-on-one battle between pitcher and batter that greatly appealed to my elevated sense of competition.

We usually played two games a week but that wasn't enough baseball for me and my buddies in the neighborhood. We'd organize our own games and play in a vacant lot across the street from the Challys' house, using a metal bat and a tennis ball, which flew a lot further than a hardball and had the added benefit of not breaking any windows in the neighborhood.

This was sandlot baseball at its purest level—a bunch of kids getting out there and playing without adult supervision. We usually had six players—including the three Chally brothers—playing three to a side. Two giant trees in left center field and right center field were our outfield "fences": hit a fly ball past the tree or high into the overhanging branches and you had a home run. Fair territory ran from left center field to right center field, which was patrolled by the two outfielders. A pitcher lobbed the tennis ball toward the hitter to start the action. We played "pitcher's hand," which meant if an outfielder picked up a ground ball and fired it back to the pitcher before the batter touched first base, he was out.

I was a natural right-handed hitter—I threw the ball with my right hand—but one day I noticed that the distance from home plate to the tree in right center was shorter. The thought dawned on me that I could hit more home runs if I batted left-handed. I jumped over to the left side of home plate, and on the first pitch, I crushed the ball and hit a long home run.

As we got older, we took our pick-up games to nearby Davenport Elementary School, where we had a backstop, a home plate, an infield, and a short fence in left field that invited right-handed hitters to swing from their heels. Sunday afternoons were a great time to play because we had Little League baseball games and practice during the week as well as Awana at church on Wednesday nights.

We played "real" baseball—using a hardball—but the pitcher was just lobbing the ball up there to let the batter hit it. Since we never had enough players but were using the entire baseball diamond, we continued to play "pitcher's hand." I didn't hit many home runs, but when I did hit a round-tripper, it was always a thrill. I loved making my home run trot, pretending I was rounding the bases at Busch Stadium, home of the Zobrist family's favorite team—the St. Louis Cardinals.

Every summer some of our extended family and some of my best friends growing up, including Jason Miller, would drive three hours from our hometowns in central Illinois to the "big city" of St. Louis to take in a couple of major league baseball games. The long weekend was part summer vacation trip and part reunion for a family tribe that was established when my great-great grandfather

Jakob Zobrist immigrated from Switzerland in 1867—right around the time that baseball was becoming popular and starting to form professional teams.

It took a lot of guts for my great-great grandfather to leave the old country back in the day. A trans-Atlantic crossing was no picnic, and neither was getting settled in a new land where everything was different—language, culture, and topography. There were no towering, jagged peaks in the Midwest.

Jakob and his family settled in the verdant flatlands of Morton, Illinois, to farm, milk cows, and make cheese. Looking back over the last 150 years, I can trace my genealogy in this fashion: Jakob had a son named Noah, who had a son named Alpha, who had my father Tom. I came along on May 26, 1981, the second of five children: I have an older sister named Jessica; a younger sister named Serena; and two younger brothers, Peter and Noah.

Dad needed the assistance of my mom, Cindi, to bring me into the world, of course. The timing of the way they met really shows how God orchestrated these events because if they didn't happen in a certain order, they wouldn't have gotten together.

On Monday, March 15, 1976, Dad was a high school senior at Morton High School. That morning he was in St. Louis, undergoing a physical as part of his enlistment into the U.S. Air Force later that summer. His family would have been strapped sending him to college, so joining the military made sense. Plus, he was ready to try something else in life.

Four days later, on Friday night, March 19, Dad took Cindi Cali out to the Sea Merchant restaurant and then a movie. They had a great time and liked each other's company. Cindi was also a senior at Morton High, and this was their first date. They made plans to see each other the following weekend.

On Monday evening, March 22, my mother-to-be was over at the house of her best friend and fellow cheerleader, Crystal

Ackerman, who talked to her about what it meant to have a personal relationship with Jesus. Crystal had been witnessing to my mother since the summer when they were roommates at a cheerleading camp. This time when she heard the gospel presented, she believed in Jesus Christ as her Lord and Savior.

The next day at school, Mom told my father that she had placed her faith in Jesus and wanted to serve Him now. If he wasn't interested in doing that, then she didn't want to date him anymore.

Mom was just a day old in her faith, but she had a fervor that my father could not deny. My dad said he needed some time to think about it, and she agreed to keep seeing my father—but only on double dates with Crystal and her boyfriend, Barney Perkins.

Those double dates happened to be to Bible studies, Youth for Christ events, and Christian concerts. Slowly but surely, my father was exposed to more of the gospel. At an outreach rally on May 21, David Wilkerson, an evangelist and author of *The Cross and the Switchblade*, said that it took more than belonging to a church to follow Christ—it took commitment. That commitment involved a life of self-denial, taking up a cross, and living for Him.

My father heard the invitation and felt like he needed to make that commitment. He whispered to my mother that he was going forward, and she said she'd go with him. Hand in hand, they walked together to the front of the church, where my father prayed to receive Christ into his heart. What an emotional moment for the both of them, which they have never forgotten.

Then there was that other commitment that Dad had made—enlisting in the Air Force. When he left Morton for basic training at Lackland Air Force Base in San Antonio, Texas, the distance between Texas and Illinois pulled him away from his old friends and his old lifestyle. Dad was a partyer in high school, a guy who drank to get drunk on weekends more times than he cares to remember. He gave that all up when he purged himself from his old friends after becoming a Christian and joining the Air Force.

Years later, Mom heard some of the drinking stories about my father. One time she told him, "I never would have gone out with you if I had known what you were like."

"Well," Dad said, "that was part of His plan. God shielded you from that so that you did go out with me, and that's how I eventually got saved."

While with the Air Force, Dad got involved with the Navigators, an interdenominational discipleship training organization that equips Christians for a life of faith. Even though they were living in different states, Dad and Mom grew closer and closer. Dad asked Mom to marry him in December 1976, and they were wed a year later on December 17, 1977, in a local church in Morton.

When Dad's four-year commitment to the Air Force was over, they moved back to Morton, where Dad got involved with the family construction business. The economy was hit hard in the late 1970s and early 1980s—high inflation and high interest rates. There weren't many houses to build, and Dad had four mouths to feed following the birth of my older sister, Jessica, and myself.

A guy who Dad knew at their home church was on the board of trustees for Calvary Bible College in Kansas City, and he thought my father had gifts that God could use in ministry. "You should think about becoming a pastor," this fellow said. His church pastor and elder said the same thing to my father.

Dad prayed about it and felt God was leading him to Bible college. Fortunately for him, he had the G.I. Bill in his hip pocket after serving in the Air Force, so we moved to Kansas City. I was four or five years old at the time.

It was at this time in my life when I first remember hearing about the gospel from a Sunday school teacher. The part that really got my attention was when the teacher said that if you did not accept Jesus Christ as your personal Savior, then you would go to hell when you die.

I had heard about hell. That was a hot, hot place where you didn't want to go. That night, I talked to Mom about what the teacher said and said I was scared. Mom told me that if I ask Jesus into my heart, then I didn't have to be afraid anymore. So that's what I did. That event happened so early in my life that I don't remember *not* being a Christian.

After Dad graduated from Calvary Bible, we moved back to Morton, where Dad did an internship at Grace Bible Church in Washington, Illinois, about ten miles away. When his yearlong internship was over in 1988, the congregation at Liberty Bible Church in Eureka, twenty miles from Morton, asked him to be their pastor. Twenty-five years later, he's still ministering to his flock.

Eureka was a great place to grow up. This small farming community has two stoplights, a courthouse, a compact downtown, abundant parks, and a private institution of higher learning known as Eureka College. President Ronald Reagan is the most famous graduate of the school, earning a degree during the Great Depression in 1932.

My parents were godly parents who poured themselves into their five children as well as their church members. I never felt any extra pressure being a "preacher's kid," although my parents used to joke that they had eyes everywhere in Eureka.

All five of us were good kids, well liked by our teachers and administrators—after I learned not to push past classmates at lunchtime. Not that I wasn't still competitive. I was always the first one to finish my tests in class, even though Mom told me that I didn't get any extra points for handing in my test before anyone else.

That competitive streak reared its head in the Awana program every Wednesday night at church. Awana is kind of like a Cub Scout/Girl Scout program where youngsters learn about the Bible and memorize verses that earn them patches for their red Awana vests.

Of course, I memorized dozens of verses to earn tons of patches. Of course, I went through my Awana book a second and third time and earned a series of review patches. Of course, I won the "Awana Olympics," where I ran laps around the Awana circle and made a headfirst slide to knock the pin over in the center of the circle. I had the fastest time because I had this burning desire to be first in whatever I did.

Of course, I won the gold medal.

* * * *

One time when I was eight years old, I saw Dad on the living room floor doing sit-ups before he went out and jogged past nearby cornfields and wheat fields. He seemed really intent on what he was doing, which meant I should be intent and purposeful as well.

I could do sit-ups. I started counting off sets of twenty before I went to bed each night, and quickly worked my way up to a hundred sit-ups. One time Dad came into my bedroom as I was knocking off my last set.

"Nice job, son. Why are you doing so much exercise before going to bed?"

"Because I want to be strong," I said. "I want to be in shape."

I was always a self-starter. Coaches didn't have to push me to get better. I was constantly asking coaches or teammates to hit me extra ground balls so I could get more glove work in. I wore out my coaches' arms with extra batting practice. I'd hit or field until my coaches said it was time to call it a day.

I was just as determined in the other sports I played growing up—junior football, youth soccer, and biddy basketball in Eureka. I even ran cross-country and track; in seventh grade, I set a school record in the mile with a 5:01 (I really wanted to beat five minutes) and would set another record with a five-foot, six-inch high jump.

Going into high school, I was one of the smallest kids in my freshman class—five feet, five inches tall and weighing a buck-twenty. I could still play good baseball, though. I made the varsity baseball team and used the experience to get better.

Things changed when I hit my growth spurt in my junior year. I sprouted to six feet, one inch and weighed a bit more than 150 pounds. I was a pitcher and a position player who could hit the ball, so I played every inning. I was also a good basketball player on the varsity team—a starting point guard who helped run the offense and made my share of open jumpers.

By this time, we had moved to a two-acre property just outside of Eureka, where my best friend Jason Miller and I helped Dad build our "Field of Dreams"—a Wiffle ball diamond in our backyard. We used white spray paint for the foul lines, lined the outfield with garden fencing we bought for cheap, dug holes in the grass for each base and home plate, piled dirt for a small mound with a pitching rubber, and planted a flagpole beyond the center-field fence. Dad even went to Home Depot and bought twenty-foot poles that we topped with bright lights. All we had to do was run an extension cord from the house, and we had the only Wiffle ball field lit for night games in Illinois, perhaps the entire country.

We cut up old bed sheets and used them to cover the lat-ticework of the rusty iron fencing. Then I spray-painted "Alpha Memorial Field" on the bed sheets after my grandfather, who passed away when my dad was only nine years old. I never got to meet Alpha Zobrist, but I thought naming the field after him was a fitting tribute for a family member who always loved baseball.

Now that we had our field ready for play, my buddies and I formed the Wiffle Ball '99 League that consisted of four teams with five guys on the roster. Ryan Mitchell and I were appointed co-commissioners. Every guy had to pay $10 to play in the league, which went toward the cost of uniforms. Yup, we had team uniforms (T-shirts) and league rules, and before games, I took my time mowing the field just so. I mowed in straight lines from north to south—home plate to center field.

We had double-elimination tournaments in the summer, and our night games were spirited, as you'd expect when you put ten testosterone-filled high school boys into a small backyard field. One time, I was pitching to Ryan Mitchell when he flicked his wrists and homered over the left field fencing.

As Ryan rounded the bases, he broke one of baseball's unwritten rules—he tried to show up the pitcher. He talked trash the entire way and suddenly veered off the base path and rapped me on the back of the head with his hand. I was wearing a cheap plastic helmet with a St. Louis Cardinals logo, so his tap didn't hurt anything more than my pride, but it still stung.

"I dare you to step over the line!" I yelled as Ryan rounded third base and headed toward home.

After he touched home plate, Ryan stepped over the line and said, "What are you going to do about it?"

I charged Ryan and pushed him through a piece of garden fencing lining the backstop. I was dusting my hands and walking back to the pitcher's mound when he got up and jumped on my back. Suddenly, we were in the midst of an old-fashioned, bench-clearing baseball brawl. No punches were thrown, but I wasn't going to let Ryan get off the ground. We wrestled for a few minutes until my teammates pulled me off the pile.

I straightened myself up, and we shook hands because it was over. But I made my point: No one was going to beat me, not even in a baseball brawl.

Sports and competition meant everything to me growing up. Sports were what I was emotionally attached to. Sports were what I was most in love with. It didn't matter *which* sport I was playing, but I was consumed with winning and out-performing the next guy. Quite frankly, sports were my idol.

Little did I know that God would take sports away from me—and give it back in the most unexpected way.

THE VIEW FROM
THE BLEACHERS

JULIANNA

Everything you need to know about my childhood can be summed up by where I sat in our family Suburban.

With two adults, six kids, and eight seats, everyone had their place. I knew mine: the middle seat in the third row way in the back. I still have a few black-and-blue bruises from the elbows inflicted on me by Caroline (who sat on my left) and Jonathan (who sat on my right).

Mom and Dad assigned me the middle seat because I was the peacemaker and got the glory of sitting between two younger siblings who mixed like oil and water. My parents knew I wouldn't fuss about taking the worst seat in our white Suburban—even though I outranked Caroline and Jonathan in birth order as the fourth of six children from the union of Jeff and Cheryl Gilmore.

My older siblings were Liz, Rosie, and Jeff, whom we called Jeffrey Paul to distinguish him from my father.

My parents sometimes called me by my first and middle names—Julianna Joy—because I was a happy kid growing up. I didn't fuss; I did my best to fit in. I was the cooperative child who went with the flow of whatever was happening. If it ever got quiet in the car, which wasn't often, I'd yell out, "Let's laugh!" I wanted to be the instigator of joy and fun, living up to my middle name.

We took long driving trips several times a year, and it wasn't uncommon for me to get into the fully loaded Suburban having no idea where Dad was taking us. After a couple of hours on the interstate, I'd look up from the book I was reading and say, "Where are we going?" I didn't have a care in the world after I found my own little zone back there in the middle seat. All I knew was that I had the right clothes and enough books, so I was ready to go.

I got my love for reading and for music from my parents, who met at Louisiana State University in Baton Rouge in the early 1970s. They both grew up in bayou country: Jeff Gilmore was from Metairie outside New Orleans, and Cheryl Kauk was raised in Baton Rouge.

A saxophone brought them together.

Dad was a pre-med student who played the saxophone in the LSU Tiger Band at football games and for a jazz ensemble that filled their drafty basketball arena with good ol' New Orleans jazz numbers. Dad still talks about sitting behind the basketball goal and playing with the pep band when Pistol Pete Maravich was scoring all those points for LSU.

Dad was a junior when Mom enrolled at LSU. She, too, was musically inclined, a total musician who could play every instrument and sing every note. (Her brother would become a keyboardist for Madonna.) After the football season, Dad decided that getting a good grade in organic chemistry was more important than playing in the pep band, so he dropped out of band.

He left his saxophone in the jazz ensemble room, which was up three flights of stairs in the main music building. This was important, as you will see.

Mom heard about the opening on the jazz band and was invited to join. After lugging her saxophone up and down three flights of stairs for practice, she saw a sax standing in a corner. "Whose sax is this? Can I use it?" she inquired.

"That's Gilmore's," someone said. "He won't mind."

Mom left her saxophone downstairs and brought her mouthpiece with her. She used my father's saxophone without ever having met him—or asking his permission.

One time, Dad went to the jazz band room and noticed that his sax wasn't in the usual place. He opened his case, where he saw a handwritten note:

Jeff, thanks for the saxophone.
Cheryl

Someone was using his sax without asking him? Jeff Gilmore was going to get to the bottom of this. He marched down three flights of stairs into the Band Room to find this Cheryl and give her a piece of his mind.

He found her all right—and his heart melted on the spot. He was smitten by her beautiful smile, big blue eyes, long blonde hair pulled back, and her cute figure. She used to be a "live model" in the window displays of various department stores in Baton Rouge, holding her pose for as long as she could before striking a different stance. I've seen pictures of when Mom was modeling, and she was gorgeous!

Dad asked her if she would like to go out with him on the spot. Their first date—that night—was at the local roller-skating rink.

Over Cokes afterward, Dad talked about how three months earlier on December 31, 1971, at 11:45 p.m., he had accepted Christ into his heart following a Crusade for Christ conference hosted by author and speaker Josh McDowell.

After quoting liberally from McDowell's book, *Evidence That Demands a Verdict*, Dad asked, "Cheryl, would you like to make that wonderful decision of knowing Christ personally?"

My mom smiled. "Three weeks ago, someone from Campus Crusade took me through the Four Spiritual Laws at the Student Union, and I trusted in Christ then."

They continued dating. Just before the end of the spring semester, Dad took her out for a nice dinner and a concert. They had a great time and returned to their hometowns for summer jobs.

My dad kept checking the mail each day for a thank-you note. His mother had raised him in a home where when you were invited for the evening, the proper thing to do afterward was to send a gracious, handwritten thank-you note. That included dates.

When my father did not receive a thank-you letter from my mother, he assumed that she did not like him. He was trying to forget her when he ran into Mom after returning to school that fall. Their conversation was awkward. Mom said something about how they had a wonderful time together and was hoping to hear from him again . . .

"I thought you didn't like me because you didn't write a thank-you note," Dad said.

As soon as the words came out of his mouth, Dad realized how ridiculous he sounded. Then my mom put her hands on her hips. "You mean that you didn't call because I didn't send you a thank-you note? But I totally like you."

That's all my father needed to hear.

Their romance was full speed ahead until another bump in the road popped up the following summer. That's when Dad decided after one year of medical school that God had called him into the ministry. As vocations go, church pastors earn considerably less than medical doctors.

Dad explained that God's call to go into full-time ministry was evidently clear to him. He could not ignore that call. Mom, however, became angry. They had been talking marriage, and now this. "I did not choose to marry a pastor. I did not sign up for this," she huffed.

My father, looking back, wished that they could have had some sort of counseling, where someone had the wisdom to tell him that he could become a doctor and view that as a ministry opportunity, but that didn't happen. Instead, he interviewed at Dallas Theological Seminary, where he was asked what he planned to do after he graduated.

"Anything but speaking," Dad replied. Dad was terrified of public speaking and thought he would be better suited in the classroom as a professor.

Meanwhile, Mom eventually came around with his change of heart to pursue the ministry, and they moved up their marriage by six months and got married on December 23, 1973, at St. Alban's Chapel on the LSU campus. After honeymooning in Orlando, Florida, it was off to Dallas Theological Seminary, where Dad earned his masters in theology and accepted his first full-time pastorate at a small church in Longwood, Florida, fifteen miles north of Orlando.

The home of Walt Disney World was where I was born on October 5, 1984. I was extremely shy growing up and was incredibly content sitting cross-legged on my bedroom floor, singing for hours or writing poetry in little notebooks that I took everywhere, including the back of the Suburban. Sometimes I would draw dresses or different shoes. Other times, I would wander into Dad's office and read books I found on his bookshelf. My favorites were the *World Book* encyclopedias with forest green covers on the top and bottom. His office had pink carpet, so I would lie down and flip through one of the encyclopedias, looking at pictures and reading various things. I could do that for hours.

I was an exceptionally compliant kid. If Mom said it was time to put on my Sunday clothes and be in the car in thirty minutes, she could count on me to be ready. I did what they told me to do and didn't question them.

I wouldn't say that Mom and Dad ran a tight ship, but they were highly organized, which is what you'd have to be with six children, especially because they wanted to homeschool us during the elementary school years. Mom and Dad were greatly concerned about the moral and cultural values taught in the public schools, so Mom taught us the basics of reading, writing, and arithmetic until we reached junior high or high school. My parents wanted us to have a good Christian foundation and strong worldview before we went off into the world.

Our homeschool education began in the morning with Dad reading either one chapter from Proverbs or five chapters from Psalms while we finished eating breakfast. Then we moved to our "classroom," which happened to be in the sunroom with tables and desks. We worked on our core subjects and did our assignments. When Mom was teaching my older siblings, I had to find my own things to do. That's why I read those *World Book* encyclopedias a lot.

In the evening before bed, Dad would read a chapter from the Old Testament or New Testament and lead us in a discussion of what we just read. He even took us through the book of Revelation. I often drew pictures of what I heard, and I can remember Dad being impressed when I explained my drawings after reading Revelation. Even at age seven, I had some idea of what was going on.

The same year I turned seven, we moved to Iowa City, Iowa, when Dad was offered the pastorate at a larger church called Parkview Church, which was part of the Evangelical Free denomination. Mom put me into a private school called Heritage Christian School to see if I would like it, and I did. I loved being around other kids and sort of being my own person for the first time.

I had a schoolgirl crush on a boy named Jordan in second and third grade. We'd leave love notes in our lockers, but we rarely spoke face-to-face because I was too shy. Then Mom homeschooled me in fourth grade—I think she missed me—but I ached to see my friends at Heritage Christian and begged Mom and Dad to let me go back. I longed to see Jordan and my best friend in the whole world, a girl named Christy.

My parents acquiesced and said I could return to Heritage Christian, but Mom thought I was too advanced for fifth grade. She had me tested, and the school administrators said I could skip a grade, which I did. I was just ten years old at the start of sixth grade. I'm sure Jordan was upset that we were no longer in the same class.

Our summer vacations, or homeschool field trips when I was younger, began with us piling into the Suburban at eight o'clock at night in our pajamas. I had my pillow with me, which was useful for slipping punches between my younger brother and younger sister in the way back. Dad liked to drive all night and give us a seven-hundred-mile head start by the time we stopped for breakfast.

We racked up the miles driving to the Black Hills of South Dakota, Winter Park in the Colorado Rockies, Yellowstone National Park in Wyoming, and the Grand Canyon in Arizona. Of course, I couldn't tell you that's where we were going *before* I got into the Suburban, but I sure enjoyed arriving at our destination so that I could escape the middle seat penitentiary in the back bench.

When we weren't taking family trips, my parents sent us to church camps in the summer. I remember going to a camp with my youth group and all of my best friends and singing with the worship team. I was twelve years old, and I loved to sing.

I can't remember if this particular church camp was in the state of Iowa that year. I can't remember a lot of things about that camp, but there is an incident that happened that I'll never forget. It began when Christy and the rest of us girls were in a cabin next to a boys' cabin. The cabins were rustic and plain; they were on stilts and not very well made. There were several dozen cabins and meeting halls spread out on the wooded property; other churches had their own Christian camps going on at the same time, so we weren't the only youth conference that week.

After dinner one evening, Christy and I left our cabin and started walking toward our meeting hall, where we would sing a few songs and hear a speaker. It was nearing dusk, but it wasn't dark yet. There were gravel paths between the cabins and our meeting hall.

We heard wolf whistles and looked toward the woods. Six guys yelled some rude things and started laughing. They were much older than us, probably high school juniors and seniors. I can't recall what they said, but I remember that from a conservative Christian girl's point of view, what they were saying wasn't nice or appropriate. Christy and I ignored them and kept on walking toward the big building.

We joined our friends and sat down, but then Christy and I realized that we had forgotten our Bibles. So we ran back to our cabin, the two of us, following the gravel path. The grounds were deserted because everyone was inside the meeting hall.

Christy and I stepped inside our cabin when suddenly we heard pounding on the plywood walls, which were thin to begin with. At first I thought it was a joke or some kind of put-on, but then

Christy and I looked at each other and both got concerned looks on our faces. This was like a bad horror movie. My heart thumped faster. This was something I had never experienced in my twelve years. We had to be in some kind of danger.

The pounding stopped. After an appropriate interlude, Christy and I opened the cabin door. We didn't see anybody. We stepped outside, looking to our right and to our left when the six guys materialized out of nowhere. The only face I can remember belonged to a chunky guy with a mohawk-like haircut. I shivered because he was so creepy looking.

I got really scared. The next thing I knew, they were circling us. I was frozen with fear, not sure what to do—when Christy bolted toward the meeting hall. Nobody chased after her, but one of the boys yelled, "We're coming for you next!"

I was alone. Six boys tightened their circle, and my eyes focused on the ringleader—the heavy guy with the mohawk-like hair cut. He had a sick smile on his face. He then rushed me and pushed me to the ground as the others followed suit.

What's going on? What are they going to do to me?

Fear gripped my throat, and I struggled against arms and hands. I fought and squirmed as best I could, but they were stronger than me. Now my uncertainty turned to panic. I wanted to scream *Get away from me!* but the words wouldn't leave my throat.

I resisted as they molested me and touched me in places where no girl should be touched. After what seemed like an eternity, I felt like the Lord gave me supernatural strength as I pushed away their hands. "God help me!" I screamed.

The boy who was on top of me—I had his T-shirt in my right hand. I pulled and ripped a huge chunk of his shirt and then pushed him off. I was rising to my feet when, for a split second, we looked in each other's eyes. I saw fear there, and I think that came from God, who showed up in that moment to rescue me.

Next thing I knew, the gang turned and ran for the woods. I took this as my opportunity to escape, so I sprinted for the girls' bathroom close by.

I ran inside, heaving for air and in shock at what had just happened. My clothes were filthy from the dirt. I felt dirty. I washed my face, sobbing the entire time.

I don't know how much time passed until I heard Christy's voice yelling for me.

"Over here!" I cried out.

She was accompanied by our youth pastor. They both stepped into the girls' bathroom.

"Are you okay?" the youth pastor asked.

I didn't want to say anything. I didn't know *how* to say anything. How could I tell him what happened?

"Are you all right?" Christy asked.

"Yeah, I'm fine," I lied. I was too ashamed to admit what had actually happened. Keep in mind that I had never been told that this kind of thing could happen. I was completely unprepared because I didn't know the word *molestation* or that boys did this to girls. In my mind, I was thinking, *What did I do wrong?*

"Did they hurt you?" the youth pastor asked, no doubt checking out my dirty clothes and messed-up hair.

"No, they did not hurt me," I said, lying again. I said this because I made a very intentional decision to hide what had just happened to me.

"Do you need me to call the authorities?"

"No, I'll be fine. Really, I'll be okay. I just want to forget about this." *And I'm never going to talk about this to anybody.*

Little did I know that a seed of fear and distrust about the human race would be planted in my heart at this time.

They sought assurance a couple more times that I was okay, but I brushed them off each time. Since I was ashamed and didn't want to talk about it, I stuffed my feelings into a deep, deep place in my heart.

In the years to come, only when my feelings threatened to bubble to the surface, did I acknowledge to myself what happened that twilight evening. In the span of five minutes, I went from being a little naïve girl to a very damaged adult. I carried that burden with me, which was reflected in snippets of poetic musings into my journal such as this, which I called "Grief." A few months after the attack, I wrote this:

> *Amputation of love*
> *This grief that has struck me down to my core*
> *until I feel pain no more.*
> *Searching for joy is in vain,*
> *asking a question, just the same,*
> *of great love and great grief.*
> *All love must end in pain,*
> *and of this I fear and calculate*
> *to be lovers not solely partners is much to risk*
> *but I cannot afford to miss.*
> *Determined fear and love must walk hand in hand*
> *A luscious promise will become barren land*
> *Your absence is like the sky spreading over everything*
> *Unity is calling the alone and the lonely*
> *My only fear is in the falling.*

It would be eight years before I came to grips with the emotional pain of that day.

The person who helped me get clarity and forgive myself was Ben Zobrist.

HOME GAME

JULIANNA

During junior high, I became really interested in fashion—what I wore and how I looked. I had a thing about making sure my nail polish matched the color of my outfits, so I must have driven Mom batty with all the trips to the pharmacy.

I liked going to the local pharmacy because I could spend a few minutes thumbing through the latest issue of *Vogue* at the magazine rack. I loved looking at the latest fashions and appraising what the runway models were wearing. I knew not to ask Mom to buy me a copy. *Vogue* was pretty worldly and an expensive magazine to boot, but I enjoyed learning what was new in the world of *haute couture*.

Sometimes I drew elegant outfits and summery flower-print dresses inside a leather journal that was a special gift from my younger brother Jonathan. He's four years younger than me, but one year when I was in my early teens he decided to empty his piggy bank and buy me an embossed blue leather journal for my birthday.

"That must have cost you a lot of money," I said to Jonathan after tearing off the gift-wrap paper. I noticed that he left the price tag on. Nineteen dollars!

"I just knew you'd love it," he said.

When I wasn't drawing dresses in my journal, I was writing down bursts of poetry. I liked words and the impression they made on the page. Sometimes hours would pass by as I jotted down my introspections while lying stomach-first on my bed. In warmer times, I trundled out to the backyard, which was completely wooded. A shallow, burbling creek ran past the back of our property, which was always a peaceful setting for thinking deep thoughts and pondering the mysteries of the universe.

An old oak tree had fallen and spanned the creek. I would sit on the tree trunk and let my bare feet hang down when the water was high enough to touch. Then I would open up my journal and follow my muse.

I liked to experiment with different types of rhyming. Sometimes the first and fourth lines rhymed and the second and third lines didn't. Sometimes there were six lines of poetry but only two lines rhymed.

Nobody encouraged me to write poetry. I was always fascinated, though, with people who wrote in an inspirational way with a different vocabulary. Even though C. S. Lewis wasn't a poet, I loved reading his books and would try copying his style in short stories. Old language was very inspiring to me. I'm glad Mom made sure we read books like *The Lion, the Witch and the Wardrobe* when we were homeschooled.

Mom was also big on me playing the piano. All six of us kids had to take piano lessons growing up because Mom believed that the piano was the basis of being educated instrumentally in music.

She said that when you understand the piano, then you understood the treble and the bass clef. Once you understood those musical notes, you could basically play any instrument you wanted to, which fit Mom to a T. She could produce wonderful music from the flute, the tenor sax, and the piano.

I took weekly piano lessons and loved making up different melodies on the Steinway baby grand in the living room.

One night, Dad dropped by while I was poking around on the piano keys.

"Are you available for a special evening a week from Saturday?" he asked.

My heart leaped. I *knew* what Dad was going to say next. He would ask me out for a memorable father-daughter date at a really nice restaurant. Liz and Rosie, who'd already had their special night with Dad, told me that he'd do this right around my fourteenth birthday.

I vividly remember Dad driving us to the Lark Steakhouse on the outskirts of Iowa City. Dad was dressed in a coat and tie; I wore a knee-length dress fit for a wedding party. Inside the low-lit dining room decorated in shades of burgundy and black, the hostess escorted us to a teeny table where the plates were almost touching. This was a white tablecloth restaurant with silverware and finery.

We were handed red leather menus, and the prices for the New York Strips and the filet mignons were sure a lot higher than a Caribbean salad at Chili's. As if he was reading my mind, Dad leaned over. "Julianna, tonight is your night. You can order anything you want."

Steak is my favorite meal, so I took Dad up on his generous offer. My filet, cooked medium well, practically melted in my mouth. Between bites, we had interesting conversations about relationships with boys and what it means to date a young man in high school. I listened, but I was too naïve about boys to understand what Dad was getting at. There was a lot that I didn't understand or *want* to understand.

I was still pushing back that horrible attack at the church camp that lingered underneath my consciousness. Only two years had passed, so the memories were never far away. I never let on to Dad what I was feeling inside, though. I was still too embarrassed. Maybe what happened was my fault.

When our plates were taken away in preparation for dessert, my father cleared his throat.

"Julianna, as your dad, I want to do everything I can to help you, to love you, to support you, and to encourage you during these teen years," he began. "I want to help you be pure until God leads the individual that He has planned for you into your life."

Dad reached into his pocket and handed me a small jewelry box. I opened it up and saw a blue topaz ring that matched the color of my eyes. "It's beautiful, Dad," I said. My eyes glistened.

Dad reached out for my left hand and slipped the ring on my fourth finger. "I'm giving you this purity ring as a symbol of the promise between you and me but also between you and God to commit yourself to stay pure until the day you get married. You'll notice three steps on the left of the ring. These signify the Father, Son, and Holy Spirit. The three steps on the right are for myself, your mother, and whomever you end up marrying. This ring also represents my prayers for the young man God is preparing for you some day."

I regarded the ring on my left hand. At that moment, I felt my father's unconditional love and knew he would always be there for me.

After what I had gone through, it felt really good to trust somebody and helped me feel even more connected to Dad. I knew without a shadow of a doubt that he was a father whom I could hold as tightly to as I wanted.

BEN

I did the "promise ring" a little differently.

First off, my parents made it clear growing up that God reserved sex for marriage and that you shouldn't be playing around before you got married. Dad didn't take me out for the purity-ring-and-dinner, but when I saw kids at our high school making poor decisions in this area, I remember thinking about my future spouse and praying, *Lord, I believe and I know You have someone for me, and I don't want to jump the gun before the time is right, so I'm going to commit and choose to wait until marriage.*

I didn't have any money, so I slipped on a key ring—one of those simple split rings that you use for keys—to remind myself of the pact I made with the Lord. I wore that key ring for several years until I got an actual metal ring.

At the same time Julianna was receiving her purity ring, I was in my junior year at Eureka High. I loved everything about high school—playing sports, being part of the Fellowship of Christian Athletes huddle group, and even the academics. Up until then, I had gotten only one B in Mr. Bill's Chemistry class. I had an 89.6 after the final exam, but I couldn't persuade Mr. Bill to give me the grade I wanted by doing extra credit. That was too bad because I got as much satisfaction scoring an A as I did knocking in the winning run on the high school baseball team.

Okay, that's not quite true. But I was still competitive in the classroom, remember?

Between schoolwork, athletics, and church activities, I didn't have time to take out girls. Not that I wasn't friendly with some cuties at church or in the school hallways, but Dad always said that having a girlfriend makes your legs weak. "You won't be as good an athlete if you have a girlfriend," he said.

Dad was trying to help me not waste time on an immature relationship that wasn't going to lead anywhere. I was on board and wanted nothing to hold me back from being the best athlete I could be. Guys with girlfriends were distracted athletes, and that wasn't going to happen to me.

I had tunnel vision when the starting gun went off, the whistle blew, or the umpire yelled, "Play ball!" Competition was my idol. I *loved* the high I got from performing well on the cross-country course, basketball court, baseball diamond, or running track. The cheers from the grandstands and the "atta-boys" from my coaches and friends were addicting. Once I tasted success, I wanted more.

Sports were crowding out everything else in my life—even God.

JULIANNA

I was on a different track with the Lord: I found it easier to separate life at school from my Christian life at church. In other words, I became a spiritual chameleon, someone who could change her colors depending on who I was associating with.

I grew up going to church every time the doors were open because my father was the head pastor and I was expected to be there. I knew all the Christian lingo—"How's your Christian walk?" or "When did you get saved?"—but I was just playing to the crowd around me.

At City High, a large public school of 1,600, I donned the role of people pleaser and did my best to blend in with the student body. I certainly didn't want to get labeled as a "preacher's kid " or some fuddy-duddy. I wanted to be cooler than that.

Something happened during my sophomore year, however, that changed my thinking. My parents signed me up for a youth event called SEMP (Students Equipped to Minister to Peers) in

Chicago. Road trips to the Windy City were always fun—Chicago was a three-and-a-half-hour drive—but on this long weekend, my faith was put to the test.

SEMP counselors trained students how to walk up to people on the street and engage them so that you could share the gospel. That Saturday morning, after the presentation, the Christian band Third Day was leading worship again when something hit me dead-on. If I was going to walk up and down State Street evangelizing Saturday shoppers, then I had to decide if I really believed in what I was doing. I didn't want to approach a stranger and make a complete fool of myself.

So who was I? Was I really a Christian, someone who believed that Jesus, the Son of God, came on this earth to die for my sins so that I could have a relationship and eternal life with Him? Or was I destined to have one foot in the church and the other foot in the world? I had been straddling both realms.

I was one of those lukewarm Christians that Dad occasionally talked about from the pulpit. At that moment, in my humility, God opened my eyes and revealed to me who He is and who I am—a sinner who needed the Savior. It was time to step up and take ownership of my faith, and I did.

This defining moment in my life came at a time when boys at City High were beating a path to my locker to say hello and get to know me better.

The boys saw that I liked to laugh and have fun. Not *that* kind of fun but pure, clean pleasure. I was Julianna Joy, remember? As far as I was concerned, fun was the greatest thing ever invented. You could have a great time in life and still be a Christian.

I ended up having lots of little romances in high school. I say "little" because they never lasted longer than a month or two. Whenever things got a tad serious, or a boy felt that I was his "girl," I broke up with him.

Delivering the bad news was never easy. Guys need a reason, so I usually played the God card when we broke up, which I preferred to do over the phone. When it was time to end things, I'd wait until he called me at the house. I didn't have a cell phone in those days.

Earnest Boy: "Hi, Julianna. I was wondering if we could go to the classical music concert this weekend. You said you really like classical music."

I knew this macho football star hated classical music, but he would do anything to go out with me, even accompany me to a cello concert. After a couple of dates, I could see it wasn't working out.

Me: "This is hard for me to say, but I don't think we are on the same page spiritually. I think it would be better if we don't go out anymore."

Earnest Boy: "But I went to your dad's church once—"

Me: "That was great, but I really want somebody who's going to lead the relationship spiritually."

And that's when the young man knew it was over. Mom and Dad had talked about the importance of being "equally yoked" in a relationship, but I didn't have the guts to stick to my ground when someone who wasn't a believer asked me out the first time. So when it became obvious that we weren't meant to be, I made it about them instead of myself, which was completely unfair. I didn't have a whole lot of wisdom in those days.

The boys I was attracted to were intellectually stimulating and could talk about books, music, or movies. For the Christian guys I dated, I thoroughly enjoyed thought-provoking conversations about the Bible. No matter who I dated, though, the relationships never lasted long.

Listen, they were all good guys, but they weren't the ones I wanted to bring home to Mama, to use that expression. That's why

I really never brought any of my boyfriends in high school over to the house to hang out or have dinner with us. It was always me going over to their home or having them pick me up for dinner and a movie.

I'll never forget the time when I called up a guy I had been dating and announced that I wanted to break up with him. He didn't take the news well. The following day, he had to go to the emergency room for symptoms of a heart attack. The condition was so serious that doctors had to shock him with defibrillator paddles.

When he got out of the hospital, my sisters teased me about breaking his heart, but the root of why I jerked boyfriends around was that they didn't measure up to my father, who *was* a spiritual leader. My thinking often went like this: *Unless you're like my father, you're not a leader.*

I didn't understand at the time that there were different kinds of leaders. You didn't have to be a guy who's in front of a church congregation of a thousand people to be an effective leader in a relationship.

BEN

Until my junior year at Eureka High, I was still growing into my body. My fuel was a steady diet of warmed-up frozen pizza and applesauce because dinner was always on the run. Like I said, it was a busy time juggling everything coming at me. I was a three-sport athlete—cross-country in the fall, basketball in winter, and baseball in spring, but when my senior year came around, my longtime friends Brandon and Chris Martin told me that I *had* to go out for football. It was now or never, they said.

I had a blast playing wide receiver, defensive back, and special teams for the Eureka High Hornets. I never came off the field. I ran kickoffs back for touchdowns, caught screen passes and long bombs that I ran to the house, and intercepted balls in the air to save games.

Basketball season was even more fun. We kept winning and winning, and the whole town of Eureka got behind us, filling small gyms wherever we played, home or away. I was a starting guard and playing well with guys I had grown up playing ball with. We felt like we were kings of the world, winning every game. If you were to ask me what was my favorite sport in high school, I would have replied, "Basketball."

In the middle of the season, though, something strange happened. I started feeling anxiety. I wasn't sure what was driving this feeling of worry, but I became concerned when I noticed that I was breathing quickly and my heart was racing.

God, what are You doing here?

I had always been a confident person, so I didn't tell my parents or my friends what I was going through. I kept everything bottled inside and put on a happy face. After all, we hadn't lost a game, so there was no reason to put a damper on things. We were talking about going all the way, winning a state championship, and going undefeated the entire season.

Just before the playoffs, I was talking to the Lord about the anxious feelings I was having. Quite frankly, I was scared about my future. I had applied to only one college—Calvary Bible College in Kansas City, the same one my dad had attended. I figured I would study the Bible and see where God was leading me.

Calvary didn't have a football or baseball program, but they did have a basketball team, and the coaches wanted me to come play. I worried, though, that playing basketball at a small college program wouldn't be enough to satisfy my athletic jones.

That's when it hit me: sports had become my idol. I was *consumed* with sports morning, noon, and night and thought of little else.

The revelation caused me to hit my knees in my bedroom. I was so wrapped up with sports and my performance that I had taken my eye off the ball—which was my relationship with the Lord. It was like I didn't *trust* Him with my future.

I bowed my head and prayed. "God, You know that sports has been all-important to me. I need to take sports off the throne. I need to submit all my sports talent to You. Lord, my life is Yours, and from now on, I'm not going to be in charge. I give everything to You, including sports. You can have that too. If You want me to go to Calvary Bible, then I'll go to Calvary Bible and serve You."

In the quiet of my heart, my prayer cemented my decision to attend Calvary Bible, not to pursue sports but to pursue His Word so that He might use me. Calvary Bible College was a good school. My older sister Jessica was finishing her first year there and raved about her college experience. The thinking in my family was that she could ease the transition into college life when I arrived on campus.

Meanwhile, our high school basketball team advanced in the playoffs until we lost a heartbreaker in the state regionals. No state title.

All I had left was a ten-week baseball season. I was a pretty average baseball player my first three seasons on the varsity team, but I finally played some good ball, hitting over .400 with seven home runs in thirty games. I won nearly every game I pitched and was named first-team All-Conference in the Tri-County Conference.

Despite my strong play in the field, I wasn't recruited by any colleges. My high school baseball coach Bob Gold made a few phone calls on my behalf, but the silence was deafening.

Part of the problem is that I didn't show how well I could play until a few weeks before graduation. I'll admit that my emotions were building to a crescendo as my last high school game approached. I counted everything off: The last at-bat. The last inning. The last out. I could barely keep my feelings in check as I gathered up my bats and glove one last time and headed out to my truck.

Now that my baseball career was in the books, there was nothing I could do except take one long look at the field. I got into my 1981 Ford pickup that had six inches of play in the steering wheel. Before I switched on the ignition, tears formed in my eyes and rolled down my cheeks. I couldn't believe that I would never play a real game of baseball again. No more thwacks of the bat or throwing an overpowering fastball past a hitter. Even though baseball was a timeless game, my clock had just run out. I had played the last inning of my life, and it hurt.

I brushed away tears. I had to let go of baseball, a game I loved.

Little did I know that when I released my grip, God would return sports and the great game of baseball back to me in an amazing way.

4

THE TRYOUT

BEN

Two weeks after high school graduation (I graduated in the Top 10 in my class of 125), I was making plans to attend a five-day Bible conference that everyone in my youth group was going to. The conference would begin on a Monday night about an hour east of Eureka. This would be my last hurrah with my high school youth group before we were off to college.

Then I received an unexpected phone call from Bob Gold, my high school baseball coach. "I just heard some college coaches are holding an open tryout on Friday," he said.

"Really? Why are they doing that?"

"They probably need to fill a few holes in their roster. You should try out. I think you're good enough to play college ball. Maybe there's a spot for you on some team."

I wasn't sure what to think. College admission departments need to know by May 1 whether you're coming to their school. I had already told Calvary Bible College that I'd be there for new student orientation at the end of August.

"Where's the tryout?"

"Brimfield High. Starts at 9:00 a.m. sharp."

We played against Brimfield. The high school was thirty-five miles west of Eureka.

"Are they going to have guns there?" I was referring to radar guns that measure how fast a pitcher throws the ball.

"I'm sure they'll have guns. All the college coaches do these days."

I'd never thrown for a radar gun, so it would be nice to know how fast I threw the pill. I never for a moment thought a college coach would want me to come play baseball for his team.

"Oh, and there's one thing else you should know," said Coach Gold. "It costs $50 to attend the tryout."

"Fifty bucks? That's a lot of money to have my arm tested."

I wasn't sure whether it was worth the money or my time to attend the tryout. Calvary Bible was a done deal, and they didn't have a baseball team. It was evident that CBC was where the Lord was leading me.

As if reading my mind, Coach Gold spoke up. "Ben, listen to me. Fifty dollars is a lot of money, but you should go anyway. I know you're set on Calvary Bible, but you should give baseball one more shot. You never know what will happen."

"Thanks, Coach. Let me talk to my dad."

When I informed Dad about the phone call, he had no objection to me going to Brimfield High for the tryout, if that's what I wanted to do. "But I'm not paying the $50," he said. "If you want to go, you'll have to pay for it."

"But—"

"You think and pray about it," Dad said.

I understood where Dad was coming from. For the pastor of a small church with a second child in college, every $50 counted.

I prayed that night, asking the Lord what I should do. Then I remembered that my grandparents had given me some cash for my nineteenth birthday on May 26. I didn't have much money to my name, but I did have $50.

I called Coach Gold back and said I'd be there on Friday.

That one decision changed my life. If I hadn't paid $50 of my own money and showed up at that ball field in Brimfield, I wouldn't be playing major league baseball today. Or more importantly, met the young woman who became my wife.

On the morning of the tryout, Mom drove me to Brimfield High, where I forked over the registration fee. Before we could get going, rain filled the skies. The tryout was postponed until Monday.

The youth conference started late Monday afternoon, which complicated things. Brimfield was a good forty minutes west of Eureka, while the youth Bible conference was an hour eastward. That meant a lot of driving for my mom because I never drove my Ford pickup out of town.

"If I can't make it on Monday, can I get my money back?"

"No refunds," said one of the organizers behind the table.

I was stuck. "Okay, I'll be there," I said.

We arrived at Brimfield High on Monday morning, where I loosened up with dozens of hopefuls. We all wanted to make a good impression for the fifteen or twenty college coaches who were circulating the field. Lots of times you can tell how good a player is just by the way he throws.

"Line up behind the left field line!" yelled out one coach. One by one, we ran 60-yard dashes into the outfield, where coaches armed with stopwatches jotted down our times. I posted one of the better times, finishing in 7.1 seconds.

The next station was shortstop, where each player received five ground balls. I smoothly fielded each ball and threw darts to first base. Shortstop was my position at Eureka High, so I felt very comfortable fielding from deep short.

The batting portion was twelve swings per player. Since I was a switch-hitter, I asked if I could take six hacks on each side of the dish. I figured that it would be more impressive if I showed the coaches that I batted from both sides of the plate. Switch-hitters are versatile—and valuable to managers. I didn't hit any home runs, but I lined several ropes into the outfield and was pleased with my contact.

My final station was in the bullpen, where I got to throw ten pitches while a coach held up a radar gun behind the plate. I made sure my arm was good and warm before I rocked and fired. My fastest pitch was 84 miles per hour—good velocity for the high school level but only adequate for college ball. Okay, so I wasn't the next Randy Johnson, but I was happy with my results. Now I knew how fast I threw.

And that was it. I was gathering up my stuff and getting ready to head out when one of the coaches caught up with me.

"Hey, Ben. I just want to introduce myself to you. I'm Elliot Johnson, and I'm the coach at Olivet Nazarene University," he said, sticking out his hand to shake mine.

"Pleased to meet you," I replied.

"I heard that you are a man of God. I really respect that. I'm a believer in Jesus Christ too, and I heard that you might be going to Calvary Bible."

"That's the plan," I said.

"Believe me, I don't want to take you away from God's will for your life, but we're a Christian school outside Chicago with a good baseball program. We're looking for players like you who are good athletes and love to play the game, but also love Jesus. I might give you a call to come take a visit up in Olivet some time."

"I'd like to do that," I said. And that's how we left things.

I didn't know what to make of our short conversation. I certainly didn't want to get my hopes up since they would surely be dashed. I told Mom everything that happened as we got on the road to drive to the youth Bible conference near Normal, Illinois, in the eastern part of the state.

It was great to see my old friends as well as my father. I filled Dad in regarding the excitement at Brimfield High, saying I thought things went well and how Coach Johnson had said he might be getting in touch with me.

After dinner, the speaker introduced the theme for the week, which was being open to what God wants to do in your life.

That was interesting to hear. I was down with that.

Back home, my sister Jessica was busy writing down phone messages for me. Coaches from *five* colleges called and wanted to talk to me about playing for their school. When Mom went home early, she returned the calls since I wouldn't be back until the weekend.

Coach Johnson seemed the most interested. He explained that he was looking for one more pitcher to round out his staff and thought I would be perfect for the Olivet Nazarene team. "But we're also looking for character guys, and I would love to have a guy like you," he said. "We can take care of your schooling if you come play for us. Why don't you come up and visit? I'd like to set that up for you."

Did I hear what I thought I just heard? Was Coach Johnson offering me a scholarship to play baseball? I thought my days of playing baseball were over—but now a bona-fide college baseball program wanted me at the eleventh hour and fifty-ninth minute— and was willing to pay my way.

"When would you like me to come visit?" I asked.

"How about this week? Would Tuesday work for you?"

I told Coach that I would have to check with my parents. Turns out that Mom and Dad had a commitment that day, but Coach Gold said he'd drive me to Bourbonnais. I called Coach back and said I'd be there on Tuesday.

When I told my parents about the phone call, we were all excited by this lightning bolt from the sky. "Maybe God is opening a door for you," Dad said.

We looked on a map to see where Olivet Nazarene University was located. The campus was situated in Bourbonnais, Illinois, two hours northeast of Eureka in the direction of Chicago. Dad didn't know much about Nazarene doctrine and what they believe, but he did know they believe in Jesus.

Coach Gold drove me to Bourbonnais, which was a surreal experience. I couldn't tell who was more excited—him or me. After touring the ball field and the campus buildings, Coach Johnson sat us down in his office. "Ben, like I said before, you're just the type of young man we're looking for. On behalf of Olivet Nazarene University, I would like to offer you a full-ride scholarship to play baseball for us."

A gigantic grin came across my face. *A college scholarship that paid for my tuition and room-and-board to play baseball?*

This was unbelievable. The only discordant note was that Coach Johnson wanted me to pitch, which was all right, but I thought I was a better hitter and fielder than a pitcher.

Where I played was a minor quibble. At least I got a cleated foot in the door. My position would sort itself out.

I was super excited to receive the formal scholarship offer and called Mom on my cell and told her all about it on the way back from Bourbonnais. Mom listened and didn't say much, which was not like her. When I got home and gave them a pitch-by-pitch description of what happened with Coach Johnson, Dad sounded a cautionary note.

"Your mother and I want to pray about where God is leading you," he said. "And you know you need to be praying as well. I think the three of us should meet with Coach Johnson before any final decision is made."

I couldn't disagree with that. The following week, Dad drove Mom and me to Bourbonnais, where we were ushered into Coach Johnson's office. After sitting down and exchanging pleasantries, Mom asked a pointed question that she had been holding back ever since I told her of the scholarship offer: "Coach Johnson, you've never seen Ben pitch or play in a game. How do you know he's worth this much money?" Tuition and fees were close to $25,000 a year, and when you added room and board in a dorm, the total amount topped thirty grand.

Mom was worried that Coach Johnson would expect too much—and be disappointed when I didn't pitch a perfect game every time I took the mound or bat 1.000 if I got to play in the field. She needn't have worried.

"Ma'am, I've coached baseball for many years," Coach Johnson replied. "I've seen Ben's curve ball, and I know he can get college players out with it. I also see your son's desire to glorify God with whatever he does."

We asked about Olivet Nazarene's spiritual reputation and heard that the school was a member of the Council for Christian Colleges and Universities, which meant it was a "Christ-centered" school rooted in the historic Christian faith. Professors and administrators had to sign statements professing faith in Jesus Christ. From an academic standpoint, Olivet Nazarene's under-graduate enrollment of 3,000 attended a fully accredited liberal arts university offering more than one hundred areas of study. Olivet Nazarene was not an NCAA division school, however.

Their athletic teams played in the NAIA, which had different eligibility requirements.

Dad asked if we could have an hour to discuss the situation.

"Take all the time you need," Coach Johnson replied.

We drove to a Cracker Barrel restaurant near campus to grab something to eat while we discussed what to do. Remember, all this was transpiring in late June, a month after high school graduation.

As we hashed out the pros and cons, Mom started crying. "I thought you were supposed to go to Calvary Bible College with Jessica," she said, dabbing her eyes. "Maybe this is happening too fast for me."

I didn't know what to say—or think. Then Dad put down his hamburger and met my eyes. "Son, you've been praying about this. You're a young man now, and you need to decide what you believe God wants you to do. I can't make this decision for you."

I didn't know it at the time, but Dad was being very wise. He knew if he forced his will on me, then I might resent what he did— especially if I didn't choose the college he thought I should attend. But I also knew Dad had my best interests at heart and had never steered me wrong in the past.

"Dad, I'm willing whatever you think I should do," I replied. "If you believe it's right for me to go to Calvary, then I'll go to Calvary. I trust your judgment."

In other words, I was willing to submit to his authority. He was my father, the head of the family. But Dad would have nothing of it. "Ben, this needs to be your decision."

I took in a deep breath. I knew what my gut was saying and where I felt the Lord was leading me. In the back of my mind, I couldn't help thinking that after I gave up my desire to play college baseball and placed the entire situation in God's hands, He had suddenly orchestrated a way for me to continue playing baseball *and* have my college tuition and room and board paid for. Talk about rounding third base with the ball still in the outfield and the third base coach windmilling his right arm.

I exhaled. "I believe I'm not done playing baseball. I want to see what God has in store for me."

Dad looked at Mom, who nodded her assent. She saw the green light as well.

"Okay, let's do it," my father said. "You'll be only two hours from home, so that means we could come watch you play."

When we returned to Coach Johnson's office, I said, "Coach, I want to play ball for you and Olivet Nazarene."

Handshakes and words of congratulation were exchanged, and I couldn't believe how my life had suddenly changed. I called the basketball coach at Calvary Bible and told him that I was going to play baseball at Olivet Nazarene. While I could hear disappointment in his voice, he wished me all the best.

Baseball practice started as soon as I arrived on campus with fall ball. We played a few games, but mainly I did a lot of conditioning with the other pitchers. Yes, I was slotted to pitch, even though I wanted to be an everyday player. One step at a time, I figured, but I couldn't help noticing that I was fifth on the depth chart at shortstop.

Obviously, I had to get used to the way they did things on a college baseball team. I watched what the older guys did and noticed that one senior stood out as the team leader—a guy named Dan Heefner.

This guy was a rock. He was *the* guy on the team, the MVP. He had this presence about him that made you want to get in his slipstream and let him lead the way. He was coming off a monster junior season after leading the nation with 22 home runs and 102 RBIs and being named to the NAIA All-American team.

Shortly after I settled in, Dan invited me to meet him at the bottom of the main student center. I was impressed, if for no other reason than I was a lowly freshman scrub while he was the big man on campus. He soon set me at ease. In fact, we didn't talk that much about baseball. He told me that he was leading a Bible study and wondered if I would like to join the group.

I was all over that idea. As we got to know each other, he did little things to set me on the right path. We talked about what God was doing in our lives, and he asked me how the Lord was leading me. He talked about how we had to be beacons to players on the team who weren't Christians yet. Even though Olivet Nazarene was a solidly Christian school that required its students to attend chapel twice a week, enrollment was open to anybody.

That fall—the first time I was away from home—Dan invested in me . . . on and off the field. He really knew hitting and had a passion for teaching others about precise-timed wrist snaps and making every pitch count. Off the field, he discipled me. He showed me passages of Scripture that were meaningful to him. I soaked up everything I could when I was around him. He was the type of mature Christian that I hoped to be some day.

Part of that maturity, I'm sure, had to come from being married. Dan had gotten hitched the previous December—and was the only married player on the team. No wonder why he was so levelheaded and responsible.

I enjoyed meeting his wife, Liz, who seemed to be as warm and friendly as Dan. They had grown up in the same church together and were high school sweethearts. They were attending the University of Northern Iowa, where Dan was playing baseball, when he decided to transfer to Olivet Nazarene so that he'd get more playing time. Their separation confirmed in their hearts that they were meant to be. Six months later, Dan asked Liz for her hand in marriage.

They were joined in holy matrimony during their Christmas break on December 17, 1999, at Parkview Church in Iowa City,

Iowa. Liz, bedecked in an eyelet wedding gown, walked down the center aisle on the arm of her father, Jeff Gilmore.

Waiting in the front row was Liz's mom, Cheryl, and two brothers and three sisters dressed in their best for the momentous occasion.

One of those sisters was named Julianna.

FIRST SIGNALS

BEN

You know how I mentioned that Dan Heefner invited me to meet with him after I arrived on the Olivet Nazarene campus?

Actually, he had to ask me several times because I blew him off at least twice before I finally showed up for our appointment. I guess I had something else going on. Call me an immature freshman.

Most guys wouldn't have bothered to reach out after being stood up once, let alone two or three times. Dan was different. He saw the big picture. He knew I needed to plug into somebody spiritually as I settled into college life after leaving home the first time.

I remember how he let me do most of the talking the first time we met. He patiently listened while I described my classes and how I was adjusting to dorm life and the lack of sleep. When I was finished, he opened up his Bible. "It's important to stay in the

Word when you're in college. I'd like to go through some passages
of Scripture with you. I think it would be good for us to memorize
several verses each week and then go through them the next time
we see each other."

I had probably memorized three hundred verses from my
Awana days, so learning Scripture was something I was used to and
came fairly easy to me. Maybe he'd suggest ones I already knew.
"Sure, let's do that," I said.

When we met, we would share our memorized verses and discuss how they applied to our lives. Many times, though, our conversations veered off on tangents. I remember telling Dan about a
girl at Eureka High that I was friends with. I casually mentioned
that I had been IM-ing this girl—sending her instant messages
back and forth on a computer screen. Back in 2000, instant messaging was the big computer fad before texting on smartphones
and posting on Facebook came along.

Dan stopped me. "Now wait a second. Let me see if I've got
this right. You are a Christian guy who says that you want to find a
godly wife someday, but you have a random friend who's a girl that
you IM with all the time. And you don't see the potential there for
a relationship with her. Is that the situation?"

"Yeah, but I like to hang out with her when I go back home."

Dan had the courage to call me out. "Why are you still in
contact with her? Is she still going to be your friend when you find
the woman you're going to marry?"

I didn't have a good comeback. "Maybe you got something
there," I allowed. "But doesn't everybody have friends who are girls
that aren't marriage material?"

"Think about what you just said. When you find that person
that you're looking for, and you start dating her and getting serious
with her, do you think you're going to still have a relationship with
some random girl you knew back in high school?"

I didn't have a good answer.

What Dan impressed upon me was any time you're in a relationship with the opposite sex, it needs to be intentional. It needs to be going places. Otherwise, you're both wasting your time. If I was only interested in it's-nothing-serious relationships, then I was sending signals that shouldn't be sent.

I thought about what Dan had said and decided that he was probably right. I was transmitting certain cues to that girl back in Eureka. I might have thought I wasn't flirting, but I probably was. And in her way, she was flirting with me. Otherwise, why would we instant message each other for hours at a time?

Dan drilled down. "Look at it from the other side of the coin. What if your wife-to-be had a close guy friend from high school that she wanted to keep in contact with? Would you like that?"

"Honestly, no. I wouldn't like that."

"Then there's your answer."

Dan became a mentor who got me thinking about my future by asking good questions like that. He showed me that the decisions I made today would affect who I'd become down the road. I took every opportunity I could to soak up his insights.

I loved it when Dan invited me over for dinner. He and Liz were living in a little apartment off campus, so it was nice to get a break from dorm food. Liz cooked a wonderful lasagna the first night I came over.

It was fascinating to watch how they interacted. Hanging out in the kitchen, they shot the breeze with each other so naturally. They laughed and teased each other. They made life fun.

Wow, this is what marriage is supposed to look like.

To Dan, she was the queen. He always talked positively about Liz when we met at the café and how awesome their marriage was. For a royal subject, she wasn't above doing grunt work. Besides cooking for him, I saw her accompany Dan to the batting cage after practice and put ball after ball on the T so Dan could get in some extra swing work. On Saturdays, Dan and I would go to the ball field and pitch BP to each other. Liz was out there shagging balls in the outfield.

They were a great example to me, and I filed away what I witnessed in their marriage.

JULIANNA

I was starting my junior year at City High when Ben enrolled at Olivet Nazarene. My big interest was music and singing. I began taking vocal lessons in seventh grade with Mrs. Bergman while continuing my piano lessons with Mr. Michelson. As I entered high school, Mrs. Bergman introduced me to Italian arias, which, as you might surmise, are sung in Italian. An aria is typically a solo lyrical vocal in an opera. A lot of times in my music book, the English translation was printed underneath the Italian lyrics so I would know what I was singing about.

Mrs. Bergman coached me on how to relax my muscles so that I could hit the really high sections. She had me lie down on the floor and sing or made me bend over at the waist and sing with my head upside down. She made practice fun, and I really enjoyed singing Italian arias and holding the big notes.

A subtle shift was happening: I was starting to love singing more than playing the piano. Don't tell Mom, but when I would go to my piano lessons with Mr. Michelson, I would ask him if he would play the songs I would be singing in church so I could practice my vocals. Then he'd also play fun pop tunes from Mariah Carey or Celine Dion and give me a chance to imitate those great vocalists. I must have sung "My Heart Will Go On" from the movie *Titanic* a dozen times.

Each run-through was a blast.

BEN

After my first semester at Olivet, I decided to do something that few guys my age did: keep a journal.

I'm not sure why I decided to jot my most innermost thoughts on the lined pages of a spiral-bound notebook, but something must have prompted me to do so. Maybe it was because of what Dan said about relationships or the way he and Liz modeled a Christian marriage. Perhaps I was a bit of a romantic myself. At any rate, here's my first entry from January 30, 2001:

> To the woman I will be in love with for the rest of my life, my future wife.
>
> At this time in my life, I might know you or I might not know you yet. But God has laid it on my heart to let you know from now on that I promise to honor and cherish you for the rest of my life, and that's a promise.
>
> Since I first took interest in girls, I have longed for something that goes far beyond the world's love. I long for a love that transcends the very emotion or that feeling that love creates. I don't claim to know much about it, but I know Someone who does know all about it. My God will be able to write a love story for us that the world can only hope to dream for.
>
> I know this only because God will be at the very core of our relationship. He will be the glue that holds us together. You ask me, how do I know our love will last. Our love can last only as long as God is alive in our lives. We'll be able to withstand the most fearsome storms that may come upon us. I can only be in awe when I think about the woman that God has prepared for me, a woman so full of virtue that none can compare.
>
> I love you already with all my heart, this is a love that's never ending. I promise from now on to hold myself true to you forever.

Love always, and forever,
Ben

Just like a Nicholas Sparks novel, right? Keep in mind that I was nineteen years old and feeling that God had a plan for me—and that plan included finding a wonderful wife to share my life with. Of course, I would never share this with any friends or teammates and risk being made fun of for the rest of my life.

During spring break of my freshman season, the baseball team flew to Daytona Beach to play a series of games along Florida's east coast. It's always freezing cold and rainy in Illinois in the middle of March—not good baseball weather.

Liz's younger sister, Rosie, flew in from Iowa to get out of the wintry weather. Like her older sister, Rosie was a looker and strikingly beautiful as well. We had a friendly introduction at the team hotel, where I learned that she was a junior at the University of Northern Iowa but just a year older than me.

Over the next few days, I noticed some of my teammates hitting on Rosie, trying to find a way to talk to her. Dan good-naturedly fended off the swarm, telling them to give Rosie her space. It was all in good fun.

One night, I was enjoying dinner with Dan, Liz, and Rosie—I could see the jealous looks from my teammates in the other booths—when Dan leaned in. "Hey, Ben, did I ever tell you that Liz and Rosie have a younger sister?"

"Ah, no." I was suddenly tongue-tied. Liz and Rosie were certainly beautiful, so if there was a younger sister in the equation, she had to be drop-dead gorgeous too.

"Her name is Julianna."

"Julianna? That sounds like a nice name."

I don't remember anything else being said, but on the plane flight back to Chicago, Dan called me over to sit next to him and

Liz. We were chatting away when out of nowhere, he turned away from me and looked toward his wife. "Hey, Liz. How's Julianna doing?" he asked.

Like she would know. Liz had been in Florida for ten days, just like me.

"I'm sure she's doing fine," she replied.

Dan kept up the cunning conversation with Liz. "What do you think about Ben and Julianna?" He spoke as if I was ten rows away and out of earshot.

Liz smiled. I think she knew that I knew Dan was toying with me. "Yeah, maybe," she said.

The embarrassing subject got dropped quickly, which I was thankful for. But hearing that Liz and Rosie had a younger sister . . . got my imagination working. What was she like? What did she *look* like? Was she as nice as Liz and Rosie? I kept those thoughts to myself, though.

Dan and Liz had me over for dinner a couple more times that spring, and sometime during the evening I could count on them teasing me about whether I would be a good match for Julianna. I played along, but the only information I could pull out of them was that she was a couple of years younger than me—and a junior in high school. My initial reaction was that a high school junior was a little young for a college freshman.

Like a moth drawn to a flame, though, I had to find out more about this girl. I wouldn't say the suspense was killing me, but I was more than intrigued.

Toward the end of the school year, when I knew Dan would be graduating and he and Liz would be off to their next adventure, I muscled up the courage to ask Dan for Julianna's e-mail address. Man, this was uncomfortable.

"I don't know it, so I'll have to get it from Liz," Dan said, which only increased my discomfort.

The next time we met at the little café, Dan pushed over a Post-It note. Printed in block letters was this e-mail address: jjoyg4@aol.com

The letters had to signify something . . . jjoyg . . . what did that mean? And the number 4?

Now I was more intrigued than ever.

JULIANNA

Liz called and told me that she had given my e-mail address to a freshman that Dan played baseball with.

"What?" I blurted. "I'm in high school. You gave a college boy my e-mail address?"

"Listen, he's really nice. Dan thinks very highly of him."

"What's his name?"

"Ben Zobrist."

I'd never heard of anyone with a last name starting with Z.

I can't remember if I was in the middle of another one of my two-month dating relationships or not. Not that it mattered. This Ben Zobrist was a long, long ways away—in another state, at a college. But if Liz thought it would be all right for him to contact me, then it should be okay.

I'd say that a couple of weeks passed by when I logged onto AOL and heard that sonorous voice say, "You've got mail."

My heart skipped a beat, as it had every time I heard "You've got mail" ever since Liz's phone call. This time there was a message from ben_zobrist@hotmail.com:

> I am Ben Zobrist. I go to Olivet with Dan Heefner, your
> brother-in-law, whom I play baseball with. I don't want you
> to think I'm some stalker or anything. I know Dan and Liz
> real well, and I have a lot of respect for them and their faith

in Jesus. They tell me you are a believer too. That's awesome! I accepted Christ when I was young, and Dan has
been doing some discipleship with me as well as a Bible
study with the baseball team.

I heard you are a singer and love music. I enjoy listening to
Christian music. Hope to hear back from you some time.

Ben

My first reaction was, *Wow, this guy is mature.* He must be very
serious and spiritual. That's how his e-mail came off to me. It had
its intended effect.

BEN

Yup, I wowed her with my spiritual depth all right. And now I just
laugh at my youthful pride.

JULIANNA

I had to reply to him, but I wanted to be clever:

Hi, I'm Julianna. I'm glad you said you weren't a stalker
because I totally thought you were, ha ha. That's cool that
you play baseball. My older brother plays baseball too. He
plays at the University of Iowa. His name is Jeff.

I can't remember what else I said, but I do recall typing Ben's
name into Google right away. "Zobrist" isn't a common name, so
he came right up. Actually, his father popped up in connection
with Liberty Bible Church in Eureka, Illinois. I found a picture
on the church website of the Zobrist family standing in front of a
stairwell, dressed in black. There were five children, and Ben's hair
was cut super short.

Then I found some baseball pictures. He looked better in those. I thought he looked cute.

BEN

I must have had a tight buzz. I don't recall answering her right back though. I didn't want to rush her by putting on an all-court press. The last thing I wanted was for her to feel like I was desperate or needing her full attention right away. So I waited a week to e-mail this person in cyberspace that I had never met. After thanking her for replying to me, I told her what had happened in the last baseball game. Then I ended the e-mail with this:

> I thought it would be fun to do some random questions. You can feel free to ask me anything you want. The question I wanted to ask you today is what is your favorite color? And why?

I thought we should keep things light and get to know each other in this manner. In following e-mails, I posed other questions:

What's your favorite book?

What are you reading now?

What's your favorite movie?

What TV shows do you like to watch?

I also asked her if she was reading any Christian books or what her favorite Christian music bands were to show her how super spiritual I was. I told her I liked listening to Third Day and Jars of Clay.

JULIANNA

I told Ben that I saw Third Day play in Chicago, but I didn't mention the SEMP youth conference and how that changed my life. But it seemed like we really connected quickly on a spiritual level.

That was what was so attractive to me about Ben and also scary. This guy just seemed so much older. He was able to talk to me about spiritual things, and none of the high school boys who took me out on dates were able to do that—or wanted to.

BEN

Something told me to take things slow in corresponding with Julianna by e-mail, so I would contact her once a week, maybe once every two weeks. My heart fluttered every time I received a reply from her, but I had never seen a picture of her. I guess that added to the mystery.

I didn't have much time to dwell on the situation because I had signed up for a foreign missions trip—playing baseball—during my summer break. Athletes in Action, a Christian sports ministry similar to Fellowship of Christian Athletes, was sending a baseball team to barnstorm through Mexico and Nicaragua—big baseball countries—to share the gospel after taking on their local professional teams or All-Star squads.

The furthest I'd ever been away from home was a high school trip to Oregon and our spring baseball trip to Florida earlier that season, so traveling beyond our borders to Central America for five weeks sounded like an exotic experience. I needed to get my first passport.

Once school was out, I packed up and headed to Dallas, where I met up with my Athlete in Action teammates to practice as well as learn how to share the gospel in a foreign country where there was a language barrier.

As much as I was looking forward to my first foreign trip as well as a chance to further my baseball skills, thoughts of Julianna never strayed far from my mind.

I would just have to be patient, but I'd never been the type to wait around for something to happen.

IN THE STARTING
LINEUP

BEN

I was looking forward to traveling to Mexico and Nicaragua for the ministry opportunities *and* the baseball.

You see, I became an everyday player again during my freshman season at Olivet, although when we took our spring break trip to Daytona Beach, Coach Johnson had me pegged as part of the five-man pitching staff. He always liked how I was a curve ball artist and wasn't afraid to throw the yakker on a full count.

Then we started the season, and our starting shortstop booted a few ground balls. The backup shortstop got his chance to shine, but he struggled in the field as well. Needing to plug a gaping hole in the infield, Coach Johnson turned to me. "Show me something," he said.

All I tried to do was vacuum up every ground ball that came my way and make the throws. I wouldn't say that I was the second coming of Derek Jeter, but I held my own at shortstop and helped my cause by hitting .330 from the plate. That didn't keep me off the mound, though. Coach Johnson still called on me to pitch every fourth or fifth game. I had a perfect 7–0 win-loss record.

By the end of the season, my right arm was about to fall off, but I wasn't feeling any pain. If anything, I was living a dream, playing—and pitching—so much baseball. The only bummer was that Coach Johnson didn't let me switch-hit, preferring that I hit from my natural right-hand side against right-hand pitching.

Playing in Central America would be a great way to gain valuable experience playing baseball in all kinds of conditions, from small stadiums in front of boisterous crowds to makeshift ball fields in the cow pastures of rural villages. My baseball "missions trip" was organized by Athletes in Action, a ministry of Campus Crusade for Christ (known today as Cru), which meant I needed to raise my own support. I sent a bunch of letters to everyone in Dad's church and all my Zobrist relatives and managed to raise $3,000 of support in the nick of time. That built my faith as well.

I mainly pitched and didn't get to play in the field that much, but that didn't matter much. Taking long bus rides throughout the impoverished Mexican and Nicaraguan countryside was quite an experience for a twenty-year-old who'd never traveled to a foreign country before. We'd pull into tiny villages where a ragtag team of gray-haired grandpas and their grandsons were waiting to play us. In bigger cities, we took the field against local All-Star teams who could play some serious ball.

Each game ended with one of us sharing our testimony through an interpreter who followed the team. Having grown up in the church, this was something I was totally comfortable with. I knew how to share the Four Spiritual Laws, which is the heart of the Christian message of salvation.

We had a contest on the team—whoever could go the longest without getting "Montezuma's revenge" would win some sort of prize. One of my teammates lost early when he ordered a sausage roll from a vendor at a Mexican League game—some sort of mystery meat tucked in a bun. An hour later, we were walking back to the hotel when our buddy keeled over, crying out in pain. He fell into a dirt street behind a car, which belched a steady cloud of exhaust into his face. His upset stomach was so bad that he had to be rushed to the hospital.

I did my best to stick to a steady diet of rice and beans and a few bits of chicken. I didn't win our contest, but I was one of the last people to go down with vomiting and diarrhea. With eating sketchy food and hearing constant Spanish, I'll admit to getting homesick on a few occasions. Walking into an Internet café and paying a couple of dollars to log on to a dial-up connection and read e-mails from home got me through some low troughs. But deep down, I always hoped to receive an e-mail from jjoyg4@aol.com.

I can still recall the sense of anticipation: Would this be the day she e-mails me? Or will it be tomorrow? I knew when I sent her an e-mail, she would always wait a few days before getting back to me. I understood why; I did the same thing when I heard from her. There was no reason to rush things, but I was playing a lot of games in my head because I had never met her or even knew what she looked like.

Getting to know somebody like that from a distance was kind of refreshing, though, and brought a sense of hope and newness to what could be around the next corner. I was always just excited to hear from her. We were still in the stage of getting to know each other by answering questions like "Who's your favorite music artist?" and "What kind of movies do you like?"

When I got back from Central America and returned to school in August, I was back in the dorms, but this time as an RA—resident assistant. Even though I could have had my own room, I chose to bunk with Jason Miller, my old Wiffle ball buddy from Eureka.

By this time, Julianna and I had started instant-messaging each other, which was a way to have a "conversation" without being on the phone. We didn't IM each other a whole lot, but when we did use instant message, that was fun too.

Then I asked if she could send me a picture. Remember, this was 2001, and digital photos were still a new thing. Jason had a printer, so I asked Julianna to e-mail him the photos so that he could print them off.

I can still remember the anticipation in my heart as the printer chugged to life. I first saw the hair on her head, then her forehead, followed by eyes as her likeness slowly inched its way out of the printer. She *was* beautiful! Her hair, the color of white blonde, was long and wavy, framing an open face with high cheekbones, a wide smile, and the fullness of youth. Her cobalt blue eyes captivated me.

"Dude, she's way out of your league," Jason said.

"I know," I replied meekly.

My face turned crimson, a St. Louis Cardinal red. Man, she was really good looking. I was kind of blown away. A second photo out of the fax machine confirmed how beautiful she was. These were posed high school class photos, professionally done, so the lighting was good.

The next time she was available on instant messaging, I flirted a bit with her. That was the first time I teased her with comments like, "Wow . . ." and "I wasn't expecting that."

I flirted on purpose with her because I wanted to get to know her better. Quite frankly, this was the first time I wondered if there would be something there down the road. Not only did she punch my attraction buttons, but she was a preacher's kid, just like me. I knew that on the spiritual side, she was a believer and loved the Lord. That was a big plus.

The second thing I liked about her was that she was an independent person. I could tell from her e-mails that she didn't need a guy in her life. She said she was in love with the Lord and felt called to do something specific with her life. She didn't know what that was yet, but she was fine with wherever God was leading her.

JULIANNA

At this point in my life, I felt God was leading me to Belmont University in Nashville, Tennessee. I explained to Ben that Belmont was where you went to college if you wanted to be in the music business or become a performer. If you asked me—someone starting her senior year of high school—what I saw myself doing some day, I would have replied, "I want to be a singer."

I was taking vocal lessons, singing in church, playing with melodies in my head, writing poetry/lyrics in notebooks—but singing was something I really wanted to pursue. Even in high school, I felt at home on the stage.

BEN

When I returned to Olivet Nazarene for fall ball, there was a gaping whole in our team leadership—Dan Heefner. After graduating, he and Liz had moved back to the University of Northern Iowa, where he got a job as a GA or graduate assistant coach on the baseball team. It's the lowest rung on the coaching ladder, but Dan thought he had a future in coaching baseball at the college level and wanted to pursue that. While in Cedar Falls, Dan and Liz got involved with the Navigators, not to get discipleship training but to equip young Christians on how they can share the gospel and impact others.

I hadn't been back on campus long when Dan invited me and some of the guys on the Olivet team to come to Cedar Falls for a Passion Conference called "The Main Event." Louie Giglio, a pastor from Atlanta, toured college campuses with a weekend conference aimed at helping university students experience a spiritual awakening or refocus their relationship with Christ.

The chance to see Dan and Liz *and* receive some spiritual nourishment appealed to me. I secretly held out hope that maybe Liz's little sister would come as well.

A week or two before the conference, I happened to be instant-messaging with Julianna:

"Dan and Liz invited me and some of the guys on the team to come to UNI for the Passion Conference next weekend. Are you going?"

I held my breath while I awaited her reply:

"Yes, I'm coming up from Iowa City. Maybe we can meet."

My heart skipped a beat. But *maybe*? Talk about being super casual. I tried to be nonchalant in my response:

"Good deal. I'll look for you on Friday night."

You better believe I'd be searching for this girl. I couldn't wait to meet her.

JULIANNA

I felt a sense of anticipation as well, so much so, but I wanted to have the right attitude. I wrote this in my journal on November 1, 2001, the night before the weekend conference:

Dear God,

Tomorrow is such a huge day for me. I'm going to Cedar Falls. Please protect me and, Father, prepare my heart to meet Ben.

Please help us to be totally ourselves around each other and not too awkward the first time we see each other. Have him take the initiative, to have us go out on a walk or go out to eat. God, help me not to read into things, but that what is true, I let be true, and that's it.

May I in no way flirt or lead him on, but just from the very moment You be the center of us. Take Your rightful place, God, in our relationship right away. Lord, please don't let those outside of us influence us or hype up the situation. I'm letting You and asking You to be our God.

BEN

We drove over on Friday afternoon, about a five-hour trip. I don't know how Julianna got from Iowa City to Cedar Falls, which I heard was a ninety-minute trip. All I knew was that I was excited to finally see her in person.

The trouble was that I was really feeling under the weather. For a month, I'd been fighting a deep pneumonia-like cough in my chest, and I couldn't get rid of it. I sat in the back of the car with the guys and coughed my brains out. My big hope was not getting anyone else sick.

JULIANNA

I got a ride to Cedar Falls with my sister, Rosie, and her boyfriend, Eric Hansen. I wasn't feeling too hot myself, but that was because my stomach was turning somersaults wondering who this Ben Zobrist was.

Before the conference started, we stopped at a Mexican restaurant, where my nervousness must have betrayed me. "We should pray about you meeting Ben," Eric said. "We need to pray that you will have fun, that you will feel like yourself, and that you will get to know each other."

Eric bowed his head and prayed for those things out loud in the middle of the busy restaurant. I was used to praying in public, so that was no problem, but hearing him ask God to be at my side as I met Ben made the whole thing a little more serious than what I thought this was going to be.

The three of us walked over to the Main Event conference after dinner just as the event was starting. We passed through glass double doors into the foyer of a large auditorium. I noticed young people were taking places on the floor. Apparently, there were no more seats left in the auditorium.

I glanced around for Ben. I had a vague idea of what he looked like from the website of his father's church, but that was months ago. The whole time I was completely unable to focus. In a few moments, I'd be meeting this guy I'd been e-mailing for six months. What would he look like in person? Even sound like? We had never spoken on the phone.

Then I noticed four guys pushing through the glass doors. I saw him—a farmer boy, rawboned, big and tall with a plaid shirt and blue jean overalls. *Oh, my . . . a hayseed. He looks so Podunk.*

He locked eyes and walked over with his right arm extended. "Hi, I'm Ben Kayser."

Ben . . . Kayser?

My eyes darted to a guy standing next to Ben. He smiled. "Hi, Julianna. I'm Ben Zobrist."

I exhaled. "Nice to meet you, Ben."

He gave me the lightest of hugs. "And nice to finally meet you."

BEN

Of course, I'll never forget the first time I laid eyes on Julianna. She was wearing a turquoise-colored short-sleeve shirt, skinny jeans that flared at the bottom, and New Balance trail girl running shoes. Her blonde hair wasn't done up or anything, just naturally kind of long. She didn't have much makeup on, but she didn't need any. She was naturally good looking.

We made small talk, which was interesting because I had been "talking" to this girl for months but had never heard her voice or seen her in person before. After a few moments, Ben Kayser, along with three other Olivet guys who came out for the conference—Paul Franzen, Chip Maxson, and Ryan Schmalz—said they would scout up some more seats. Turns out there were a few places left.

We walked inside the auditorium, where we took our seats. I let Julianna step into the row first, and then I took the seat next to her. I remember feeling a bit awkward sitting next to a person I had a connection with but didn't know very well.

JULIANNA

When I sat next to Ben, it all felt very intentional, like it was a setup.

Here's the person you've been destined to marry. See if you like each other.

This must be what an arranged marriage feels like. I remember looking at Ben's shoes and thinking his legs were so big. Those were really strong legs. He didn't notice me checking him out, though. He was too busy taking a lot of notes.

BEN

I may have been scribbling a lot of notes, but I wasn't remembering anything that was being talked about. My mind was running fast thinking about Julianna.

All in all, though, it was a pleasant evening. When we said our goodbyes, we made plans to see each other in the morning. We went to a breakout session together, which led right into the lunch break. I asked her if she would like to get a bite to eat. She said yes, so we found a café next door to the conference.

JULIANNA

Ben asked if we could be seated in a quiet section, and we were led to an area where there was nobody else. All the other people were seated in the main dining area, while we were led to a table behind a half wall that totally isolated us. Why did he want to sit here?

BEN

I guess I wanted a quiet place where we could catch our breath and have a relaxed conversation. We started by talking about how we grew up. I remember being surprised when she said she had no memories of sixth grade because she was never in sixth grade.

"How did that happen?" I asked.

"I skipped. I went from fifth grade in homeschooling to seventh grade in regular school because I tested out well," she said.

That meant she was a smart girl—and a year younger than I thought.

"When's your birthday?"

"October 5."

"I mean, what year were you born?"

"1984."

I did the mental calculation. I was three years, four months older than her, even though we were separated by only two grades.

"You're three years younger than me."

"Yeah, I know."

"But you're so mature."

When Julianna laughed uncomfortably, we mercifully let the subject drop. But I could see this girl was beyond her years, especially in the area where it counted most—her spiritual maturity.

Then we talked about music, and somehow got on the topic of Britney Spears.

I can't remember exactly what I said about Britney, who, in 2001, was at the height of her popularity and coming out with sexy videos and photo shoots. Her scantily clad body was everywhere, so I ripped on her immodesty in between bites of my hamburger. I probably said something like, "She's using sex to sell herself as an artist."

JULIANNA

He said a lot more than that, but it was along the themes of, "I can't believe how she dresses and what she sings about."

My thought was that Britney Spears was not a Christian. If you're a mainstream artist, like she was, then that is what you're going to look like and that's what you're going to sing about. I always had a heart for those pop artists and felt a burden for them. Hearing Ben diss her like that was a major turnoff for me. He came across like a spiritual know-it-all.

BEN

I *was* trying to impress Julianna with my spirituality, but I could tell my comments hit Julianna like a wet blanket. She probably thought I was way too strict or legalistic or something, but I noticed that she kind of clammed up after that. As lunch came to an end, the sparks weren't flying between us.

JULIANNA

I wasn't interested in Mr. Super Judgmental anymore after hearing him go off on Britney Spears. But you know, I was thinking of myself as more holy than him because I would never say anything like that. In our own ways, we were both trying to impress each other on the spiritual status ladder, but we were both doing a poor job at it.

BEN

That afternoon, we went to separate breakout sessions and then saw each other for the Saturday night meeting. I hoped that I hadn't stepped on her toes with those comments about Britney Spears, but I definitely noticed a certain coolness in Julianna's demeanor.

After the final session on Sunday morning, everyone went over to Dan and Liz's place for lunch. When we were done, I said goodbye to her when the guys and I departed for the drive back to Bourbonnais. Now that we had finally met, I still felt attracted to her and wondered if there was a future for the two of us, even though I felt like things fizzled a bit toward the end.

Rolling past Iowa cornfields, with time to think things through, I knew I had seen something special in Julianna. I continued to grapple with those thoughts over the next couple of days until I made another entry in my journal. This one was entitled, "To My Wife."

November 5, 2001

Last weekend, I went to a Christian weekend rally at the University of Northern Iowa called "The Main Event." It was a great time of refocusing my relationship with Christ to where it should be, but I think I learned so much more than that.

I met someone awesome this weekend. Who knows? It could even be you. I've gotten to know her through e-mail the past six months, and I knew I would meet her this weekend, but I wasn't sure what to expect even after knowing her well through e-mails. I got to spend some time personally with her one afternoon, and we talked about a lot of stuff.

The thing that attracts me to this girl the most is that Christ shines through her life like no girl I've ever known before. I can tell that she desires Him above all else, and she eagerly seeks Him on a daily basis. Automatically, I just wanted to know her better.

My first reaction was that I like this girl and want to see this friendship go further. But what I learned this weekend was that I must be patient. That is so hard for me. I'm the type of person that sees what I want, sees the goal, and goes and attains it. Often times in the past, however, I have tried that and forgot to ask what God wants for me to do. So I'm determined to be patient this time, even in a situation like where I know that this is the type of girl that I want to serve Christ with some day. I have to be patient and wait upon the Lord.

I have to constantly remind myself that God's will is sovereign, and if He wants it to happen, it's going to happen. I am content to be patient with every decision I make concerning this girl. That means I will eagerly and earnestly pray about her, for her, and for my own wisdom in decision-making. I understand the severity of my decisions and that I'm dealing with another person here.

Who knows? Maybe nothing will happen . . . maybe this girl I'm talking about is not you.

But . . . perhaps you are her in the future. In this case, I promise that I'm going to seek God's counsel in everything. And in this, you will know that I have had a pure heart from the beginning, that I'm being careful to consider you my wife in the future, regarding everything that will keep our relationship holy and blameless before God. I love you and know I will love you forever. Okay, maybe I still don't know you yet, but maybe I do know you now. Only God knows.

All I know now is that I promise to be patient and to be careful with every decision. I'm promising to love you now, which is a promise that will not fade away.

Love,

Ben

It's evident, rereading these words today, that I was at a point in my life where I was ready to fall in love.

I just didn't know if that special person would be Julianna Gilmore.

LONG RELIEF

JULIANNA

Ben and I continued to e-mail each other after the Main Event conference, but our contact was sporadic. I think it's because of the signals I was sending out. Maybe I took a couple of days longer to respond back to Ben. Maybe the few times when we did instant messaging, I said I had to go earlier than previously.

One time during the Christmas break, I was in Dad's office—the room with the pink carpet. He had a cherry wood desk with a big computer on it. That's where I did all my computer stuff—research for homework, sending and answering e-mails, or swapping instant messages with Ben. On this particular evening, I was checking my e-mail when Rosie dropped by with Eric, now her fiancée.

"What are you up to?" my sister asked.

"Nothing much, just going through my—"

I stopped. There was an instant message from Ben. It had been several weeks since I heard from him.

"Did Ben just write you?" Rosie had a conspiratorial smirk on her face.

"Yeah, he just sent an instant message. He's wondering how I am and says he's glad to be home for Christmas."

That gave Rosie and Eric an opening. They had taken an immediate liking to Ben and told me several times that I should get to know him better.

"That Ben needs to man up and ask for your number." Eric nearly thumped the desk with conviction.

"Yeah, you've been IM-ing for months," seconded Rosie. "What's taking him so long?"

On and on they went, heaping abuse—though friendly—on my shoulders. They were having a grand old time teasing me.

I got up from the swirly plastic chair. I'd had enough. I didn't want to do this anymore—pretending to have a "relationship" with Ben Zobrist. Whatever we had, it was over. "See you later," I said. I left his instant message on the screen.

My bedroom was next door to Dad's office. As I fell on my bed, I heard Rosie and Eric laughing and making jokes. Then I heard my sister's fiancé say, "What else should I write to Ben?"

Something was up. I hurried back in the office, where Eric was busy tapping on the keyboard.

"What are you doing?" I demanded.

"IM-ing with Ben."

"You're what?"

"Come see for yourself."

I came around the desk and looked at the screen:

Ben, this is Eric, Rosie's boyfriend. You need to man up and ask for her phone number.

"You're not going to send that."

Eric smiled and locked eyes with mine. Then his right index finger pressed the return key. "Can't stop me now," he said.

BEN

When I got the instant message from Eric, I wasn't sure what to think. Was he being put up to do this? The sparks-o-meter wasn't exactly dialed on high after the conference weekend in Cedar Falls. Sure, we had remained in touch, were still communicating, still friends, but in the back of my mind, I was wondering: *Is this going anywhere?*

I responded to Eric—and Julianna, too, since it was her e-mail address—in a noncommittal fashion: *All in good time. We'll get it figured out.* There really wasn't much more to say.

Later, I remembered Dan's words that relationships need to be going somewhere; otherwise, you're both wasting your time. I thought about what he said and determined that we had arrived at a fork-in-the-road moment in our relationship, however tenuous it was. Were we going to stay in the friend zone? I e-mailed Julianna a few days later with an important message:

> What do you think of me calling you? I want to see if this is going anywhere. I really like you, you're a really great person, and I would love to get to know you better, but I want to see what you think about this first.

JULIANNA

When Ben asked if he could call me, I knew that was something I should discuss with Mom and Dad. They talked a lot about "boundaries" and how emotions can get away from you with the guy/girl thing.

"I don't think him calling you would be a good idea," Dad said. "He's in college. He's in a different place in life than you are."

Mom was more succinct. "Oh, my goodness, he's way older than you. Plus you're planning on going to Belmont, so I don't see how that could work."

BEN

She didn't e-mail right back, which was normal. But I was dying inside, waiting to hear from her. Three days later, she finally sent this message:

> Hey, I have been praying about this the last couple of days,
> and it really has occurred to me that God is leading me to
> Belmont and that I should be putting my focus on that area
> in my life right now. I am in the middle of my senior year and
> going to college soon. I know I want to pursue music. What
> I don't want is to be in a relationship right now. I am not
> really ready for that kind of a step.

Whoa, she shot me down. Out of the sky. But now everything was cut-and-dry. I had been praying about us, asking the Lord to either set us up or cut it off. Well, now I had my answer, just as she received an answer to her prayers. I took the high road in my response:

> I'm glad you told me how you felt. This only confirms to me
> how strong your relationship with the Lord is, that you would
> pray about this. And telling me how you felt is great, so we
> should not communicate any more if we are not going to be

going anywhere anymore. I wish you all the best with whatever God has in store for you.

I did receive a gracious but short response back from Julianna
in which she said she respected me a lot for saying what I did. I
felt at peace. She was a great girl, but I wasn't the right one for her
and I guess she wasn't the right one for me. There were no hard
feelings. It was becoming more evident that if God was in charge,
then we didn't need to force something to happen.

In looking for a future wife, I felt like God wasn't going to
make me jump through a whole bunch of hoops and push over
mountains to get to a girl. He was going to bring the girl and make
it obvious to me that this was the one He wanted me to be with.

I cut communication off with her. No e-mails, no IM-ing.
When I returned back to Olivet in January, baseball practice
started anew, and it looked like it would be a busy season again.
Coach Johnson had me penciled in at shortstop and short relief.
He knew I had thrown too much my freshman year.

In March, we flew to Florida during spring break to play a lot
of baseball games and shake off the winter rust. Coach had us staying at a hotel right on the sand at Daytona Beach. After playing
our first game at nearby Jackie Robinson Stadium, we were bused
back to our hotel, still in our uniforms.

I stepped off the bus, carrying a bag of gear into the lobby.

Then I saw her—Julianna. I blinked twice, but my eyes weren't
fooling me.

JULIANNA

Rosie and I had been at the beach all day, but I had gotten sand in
my right eye while we were in the water. My irritated eye was really

bothering me. "Why don't we go inside to the restroom and wash it out?" Rosie suggested.

That sounded like a great idea. We were in the restroom when Liz popped her head in. "There's a big bus of boys that just parked out front."

"Fun!" I said.

When I walked out of the restroom, my right eye was red and puffy, I was in my bikini, and I was ready to see who were all these boys walking off the bus. They started filing out, and *Oh, my gosh. Oh, my gosh. Oh, my gosh.*

There was Ben. But I couldn't let him know that I spotted him.

BEN

Just inside the lobby, I approached her and touched her left arm to surprise her.

"Hey! What are you doing here?"

Julianna turned and looked at me. Then she broke out in a wide smile. "Ben! What are *you* doing here?"

"We're down here for our spring trip. This is the hotel we're staying at. We just got done with our first game."

"That's so funny you're here because Jeff is here playing ball too. We came down to Florida to watch him play."

"What a coincidence that you're at the same hotel as our team."

"No, my family isn't staying here, but my grandparents are. We're staying at a different hotel inland a bit."

"That's cool. Are you going to be out on the beach?"

Julianna looked at Rosie. "We'll be out there."

"Then I'll come out and say hello."

After I changed into some trunks, I found Julianna laying on a towel on top of the hot sand. Rosie was cooling off in the water.

I laid down a towel, and we caught up on the last three months. While I could see that nothing had changed about our situation, it was still nice to just see her again and hear her voice. Kicking back with her in a resort, beachy situation helped me reconnect with her dynamic personality and the fun-loving person she was. She had a way of lighting up the room, even if that room was bordered by the Atlantic Ocean, blue sky overhead, and beach hotels as far as the eye could see.

We kept the conversation light and fun, and I thoroughly enjoyed myself. I kept looking for her each time I went to the hotel lobby, but I only ran into her one more time that week. Once we returned to Bourbonnais, I knew it was time to forget about her and focus on baseball again.

I had a fantastic sophomore baseball season, batting .368 and hitting seven home runs (I only had a single round-tripper my freshman season). Once again, I was perfect on the mound with a 4-0 record, although I pitched less. My exploits on the field earned me first-team All-American honors in the NAIA division.

I wanted to play summer baseball somewhere, but nothing worked out. This was a shame because there were dozens of amateur summer leagues out there for college-aged players looking to hone their skills.

My uncle, Matt Zobrist, ran the Christian Center, a multiuse recreational center with ball fields in Peoria, about twenty miles west of Eureka. He said he could put me to work raking infields, mowing outfields, and lining baseball diamonds.

I needed to make some money, so Uncle Matt handed me a rake and the keys to a sit-down mower. When I was caught up on my work, I got a chance to throw with Brian Shouse, a sidearm pitcher with the Kansas City Royals who had played college ball at Bradley University in Peoria.

Brian treated me well and took an interest in me, as did Dave Rodgers, a longtime youth baseball coach who ran the sandlot programs. Coach Rodgers had coached thousands of kids over the years, including Joe Girardi, who was at the tail end of a fifteen-year career in the majors (and who's managing the New York Yankees presently). Coach Rodgers knew of my budding talent and was concerned that I wasn't playing summer ball and advancing my skills. The old coach took it upon himself to make a few phone calls on my behalf.

Coach Rodgers reached the manager of the Twin City Stars, part of the Central Illinois Collegiate League. He didn't short-sell me. "The boy is too good," said the coach. "He needs to be playing somewhere."

The Twin City Stars played in Bloomington, less than thirty miles from Eureka, a perfect situation for me. The manager said he had enough players, but when Coach Rodgers pressed him, he reluctantly agreed to give me a one-week tryout.

I was ecstatic to be playing again because I knew I needed to play summer baseball if I wanted to get better. My tryout lasted one night. I went 5 for 5—three hits batting left-handed and two hits batting right-handed. "You're on the team," the manager said after the final out.

I mowed outfields by day and played baseball at night. One summer evening, though, I joined a Christian Center bus trip to see a Cardinals game in St. Louis with a busload of Little League kids. Dad and Uncle Matt came along as chaperones. We sat in the cheap seats, of course, high up in Busch Stadium's upper deck. The players looked like ants from the nosebleed section, so I told Dad I was going down to field level so I could get a closer look at big league pitching. It had been a couple of years since I'd attended a major league game.

I stood behind the home plate section and checked out the arms. I felt like I was picking up their pitches pretty good, which was a revelation to me. I thought I'd be blown away by their speed or the way their curveballs dropped off the edge of the table. The opposite occurred. I could hit these guys.

When I returned to Dad and Uncle Matt, I shared my observations. "I can hit this pitching," I declared. "And if I can do that, I can play in the major leagues."

Dad and Uncle Matt didn't say anything. Perhaps they didn't want to squash the dreams of a twenty-year-old. They knew the odds of reaching the big leagues were infinitesimal to begin with and had to be even lower for someone playing at the NAIA level.

Meanwhile, I continued to hit and field well for the Twin City Stars. One night, we played against the Decatur Blues, about ninety minutes south. In the last inning, I heard the PA announcer say, "Now pinch-hitting for the Blues, Jeff Gilmore."

I wondered if this was the same guy from the University of Iowa, which could only mean one thing: he was Julianna's brother. I had to find out.

After the final pitch, I searched him out. "Hey, Jeff. I know Dan and Liz really well. I'm Ben Zobrist."

His eyes lit up in recognition. "Oh, I've heard of you."

We had a friendly conversation, and because I had said hello to him, I took the liberty to send Julianna an e-mail saying that I met her brother at a game in Decatur.

I got a response saying that Jeff was playing in my summer league and that she had seen a few games with her parents. "I'll let you know if we end up coming to a game against you guys," she wrote.

That was nice to hear. But even better news was when she wrote me a couple of weeks later:

Hey, my brother is playing you guys this week, and the town
you are playing in is a lot closer for us to drive to than his
home field, so we are going to come and see that game.
Jeff is going to be pitching in that game.

My response was short and to the point: *Awesome! I look forward
to seeing you.*

Frankly, I was surprised that Julianna was coming to the game
and that I would see her again. She couldn't be making this effort
just to see me.

JULIANNA

It was a day game on a Saturday afternoon, and I remember how
hot it was. I wore red lipstick, a white V-neck halter top, open in
the back, and cut-off jeans as a concession to the heat.

I was sitting in the stands with my parents, watching the game,
when I found out that Ben's parents were sitting right behind us
with his younger sister, Serena, who was blonde and cute. I didn't
know his parents were going to be there, and I was worried that
they would think I was dressed immodestly, wearing the V-neck
halter top.

I turned around and introduced myself, making sure to give a
very firm handshake because Dad taught me that you always grip
firmly when shaking hands, especially with men that you want to
impress. I'm sure I white-knuckled Ben's dad, who was friendly and
nice. *Nice to meet you!*

That was sure weird watching my brother pitch against Ben. I
can't remember how either of them did, but I do remember what
Ben and I did after the game. We sat on a curb behind the outfield
fence and talked for *two* hours.

My parents were parked not far away. They just sat in the white Suburban while I chatted with Ben about what was happening in our lives. They were incredibly patient.

After saying good-bye, my parents drove us to a nearby motel, where we had a couple of rooms. That night, I wrote this entry in my journal:

> *Saturday, July 13, 2002*
>
> *So I saw Ben today. I was sitting in the bleachers, looking for his sister, whom I had never met. When I saw his parents and three kids sit down, I knew it was them.*
>
> *So I went up and said, "Hi, are you the Zobrist family?"*
>
> *To my relief, it was. What fun to finally meet.*
>
> *Ben did a great job. He came up to Jeff and congratulated him and introduced himself to my dad. I thought that was cool. Ben and I talked for a while after a game, and to make a long story short, one of his good friends from AIA [Athletes in Action], Danny, is dating Lindsay [my best friend] from Belmont.*
>
> *It's a small world, huh? I might go again to see Ben's team versus Jeffrey's team in two weeks and possibly sing the National Anthem. Ben thinks I should. He's always encouraged me, even though he's never really heard me sing. Oh, well . . .*

BEN

Even though I can't remember how I played that night, I'll never forget seeing Julianna after the game.

She talked about how excited she was to start college in the fall and felt like the Belmont experience would really help take her singing to the next level. She mentioned that she had been helping some elderly people that summer and described what the Lord had been teaching her through that.

As I listened, I was more and more drawn in. This girl was awesome and an impressive person all the way around. I was getting to hear her heart, which only attracted her to me more and more. At the same time, though, I realized that nothing had changed between us.

She didn't sing the National Anthem two weeks later because I didn't see her when I played a road game against Jeff's team. But it was clear that while we were on friendly terms, there was no romantic relationship between us. When I returned to Olivet to start my junior year, I went on a few dates with different girls, but I continued to think, *You know, I don't want to get involved with a girl if I don't see it going anywhere.*

If I had one date with a girl and it wasn't good or we didn't hit it off, I was done with it. I measured each girl against my ideal sweetheart: Julianna Gilmore. She was always in the back of my mind, but I was careful not to pray for her specifically. I remember my prayer being, *Lord, I just ask that You bring the right woman into my life.*

One time, after another unsuccessful dating relationship, I e-mailed Julianna to see how she was doing. I felt she would be receptive to hearing from me because we had a nice talk after that summer league ballgame. I wanted to find out how college was going and how she felt about being on her own for the first time.

I hope everything is going well at Belmont. I was just thinking about you and was wondering how college was going so far, I wrote. I'll admit that there was an ulterior motive, which was I wanted her to know that she was still in my mind a little bit. I was curious what she would say back.

Her reply went like this: *I'm really liking Belmont. Classes are going great. I'm getting to sing a lot, and we're doing this and that . . .* and she described the exciting areas of her life.

I think I e-mailed her only three times during my junior year. I had baseball on my mind, of course, but now that I was an upperclassman, I felt it was time to step up and show some Dan Heefner-type leadership. I became the leader of the Fellowship of Christian Athlete's Huddles, the weekly Bible studies for sports-minded students, on the Olivet Nazarene campus. I invested in people's spiritual lives and did my best to make everyone around me spiritually stronger—as "iron sharpens iron" in Proverbs 27:17.

Praise the Lord, I was sharp on the ball field. I had another NAIA All-American season, hitting a team-leading .409 and making nine appearances on the mound, posting a 3-0 record with two saves and a stingy 1.66 ERA. For my efforts, I was named Player of the Year in the Chicagoland College Athletic Conference and listed as an NAIA Scholar-Athlete, so my report card was good.

My baseball skills were developing rapidly as I filled out a six-foot, three-inch frame with 185 lean, muscular pounds. I even showed some versatility when Coach Johnson suggested moving me from shortstop to second base, saying he wanted to save my arm from the long throws from deep in the hole. The only down spot was that Coach didn't allow me to switch-hit very often.

Sometimes moving from shortstop to second base feels like a demotion since shortstop is considered the most important and demanding defensive position in the field. The shortstop is often the captain of the infield and gives signals to other infielders about how to position themselves. The position demands athleticism and range, which is why some members of the Zobrist clan felt like I was too good to play second base.

I shrugged my shoulders. I knew Coach wanted to move me over to second so that we could field an improved team. So I played most of the season at second base, learned the nuances of the position, and worked on making the pivot on double-play balls. Little did I know that my flexibility on the field would serve me well when I reached the major leagues.

But my road to the majors didn't start after my junior year, when college players become eligible for the major league draft. I had heard about other NAIA All-Americans being drafted by a big league team and being signed to a minor league contract, but no team drafted me in the 2003 June draft, held shortly after my banner season. I wouldn't say my dream of playing major league baseball was finished, but the chances of ever putting on a big league uniform looked exceedingly remote.

Oh, well, I could always play summer ball. This time around, there were plenty of teams that *wanted* me to play, so now it was a matter of finding the best summer league team to be part of. One of them was the Wisconsin Woodchucks in Wausau, Wisconsin, part of the Northwoods League, a sixteen-team association that plays in small towns and cities in Wisconsin, Minnesota, and Iowa. This was a chance to play six times a week in front of baseball-savvy crowds of two or three thousand people each night, a great learning experience for college players.

The Woodchucks manager was Steve Foster, who played for the Cincinnati Reds and scouted for the Florida Marlins. After hearing about me from Dan Heefner, he put me through a private tryout during my junior season to see if I could hack it because the Northwoods League was filled with some of the best college players in the country from Division 1 schools.

The first thing he said to me after I arrived in Wausau was this: "I have no idea why you're here. You should have been drafted and playing pro ball somewhere."

Hearing him make that declaration boosted my confidence. My manager knew I was a believer—he had done some asking around, plus I attended a Christian college. Coach let me know early on that he was also a follower of Jesus.

"We have another Christian guy on the team that I want you to room with," Coach Foster said. Players in the Northwoods League stayed with host families and shared a bedroom.

"He played at Dallas Baptist this spring. Comes from a great family," said my manager.

"What's his name?"

Coach Foster didn't hesitate.

"Jeff Gilmore."

BEHIND IN THE COUNT

JULIANNA

I had more than a few boys interested in taking me out my freshman year at Belmont. One guy, however, turned out to be a bit of a rogue. On our second date, as he was driving me back to my dorm following dinner, he pulled into a deserted parking area in a more secluded part of campus.

When I asked him what he was doing, he leaned over and tried to kiss me. I slapped him in the face. "You take me back to my dorm right now!"

That was the last I ever saw of him.

At the end of the school year, Jeffrey Paul called. He said he had some exciting news to share.

"Jules, guess who's on my summer league team?"

"Who?"

"Ben Zobrist."

"You've got to be kidding me."

Two weeks later, my brother called from Wisconsin with more news.

"You'll never guess who my roommate is."

"Ah, Ben Zobrist?"

Holy cow, I couldn't get away from this guy.

I wasn't going to see Jeff—or Ben—play in Wisconsin because I was heading in another direction for the summer—Texas. I'd spotted a job posting at Belmont looking for singers to spend the summer singing on the various worship teams at the Pine Cove Christian Camps in Tyler, Texas. I applied and got hired to lead worship for the family camps. Pine Cove was a big deal, hosting more than 20,000 adults and children every summer.

Dad drove me in the Suburban to the rolling hills of Tyler, midway between Dallas and Shreveport, Louisiana. The long-distance trip was just like old times, but on this journey, I knew where we were going and no elbows were being thrown my way. We did the fourteen-hour drive in one day and had a great father-daughter stretch in the car.

The first staff member to greet us at Pine Cove was a young man three or four years older than me. I'll call him Randy.

He was engaging and personable, eager to please. Randy said he was an assistant pastor at a church on the Texas A&M campus. From his energy and leadership qualities, he appeared to be going places.

It wasn't long before he swept me off my feet. I fell for Randy—hard. And he fell for me. But Pine Cove had an ironclad rule: single pastors were not allowed to date staff members. That meant we couldn't be seen as a couple, holding hands or going on romantic walks, that sort of thing. To get around that rule, Randy suggested that we drive off campus. Many evenings when we were done with our day, we would get in his car and sneak out of camp to hang out and talk. Then we'd slip past the entrance before curfew. All very secretive.

We were off on Sundays, so we'd drive into Tyler and sit together in a Laundromat for hours, chatting while the machines washed and dried our clothes. Sundays were also the days when I made phone calls home and to my siblings, who were pretty spread out. Dan and Liz were still in Cedar Falls, Rosie and Eric were in their first year of marriage and living in Minneapolis, and Jeff was in Wisconsin playing ball with Ben. My two younger siblings, Caroline and Jonathan, were still living at home.

Eventually, I told all of them that I had met a special guy. I mentioned that Randy was involved in a student outreach ministry at Texas A&M with such-and-such church and that he was also doing a weekly radio program on the campus station. His mom was a professor at the university, but I forget what she taught. He said his sister played basketball at Louisiana State University. Randy was a fascinating guy who seemed to know everybody.

By the end of the summer season in August, we were getting serious—real serious. I'd say that we were marching toward a June wedding. He hadn't popped the question yet, but I really thought Randy was *the* man God had prepared for me.

This was the first time I really opened my heart to a guy. You see, I had a major lack of trust in men, and that began the day I was sexually assaulted at age twelve. That's why all my relationships in high school—and a few at Belmont—were short-lived. I was always looking for the moment when I couldn't trust that person anymore. I usually came up with something pretty quickly.

Being wooed by Randy was changing that, but it also helped me take my mind off a series of horrible dreams I was having about the molestation. That was a bad summer for me. Every night, it seemed like the terrible nightmares returned with a vengeance.

I didn't tell Randy about my bad dreams because I didn't want that ugliness to enter our relationship. Better to keep things bottled up and not roil the waters.

When Pine Cove was over, I had to return to Belmont for my sophomore year, and Randy had student ministry waiting for him at Texas A&M. When Mom and Dad picked me up at Tyler, I made sure we did a "meet the parents" thing with Randy. I'm sure Randy was all I talked about on the fourteen-hour drive home. As soon as we arrived in Iowa City, though, I packed up for Belmont and was off to Nashville. Meanwhile, Randy and I continued to have intense conversations on the phone, talking for an hour or two every evening.

Unbeknownst to me, Dad decided to do some research on Randy. He did so, he would tell me later, because a few things about Randy sounded off to him. Dad had attended Dallas Theological Seminary, so he knew about campus ministry at Texas A&M. The church Randy mentioned that he was associated with didn't exist on that campus. Dad confirmed this with a simple Google search.

Once Dad started noodling around the Internet, he couldn't confirm anything that Randy said. The radio program he hosted once a week was nowhere to be found. His mother wasn't a professor on the campus. His sister wasn't on the women's basketball team at LSU. Nothing checked out. Dad even called Texas A&M and talked to the person in charge of parachurch ministry. He had never heard of Randy.

Everything Randy had said about his background or present-day employment couldn't be verified. In other words, everything he told me was untrue.

I had only been back in Nashville for a week when I received a phone call from Dad. My father got right to the point.

"Julianna, you're going to have to trust me on this, but I'm exercising my fatherly rights and asking you to break off this relationship. The next time he calls, I want you to tell him that he is never to call you again, never e-mail you again, never write you again, and never try to communicate with you in any way whatsoever."

"But why, Dad? What's going on? What happened?"

"I'm not going to tell you right now. I'll tell you someday, but I've done some checking on what Randy's been saying about himself. What I've learned troubles me. It's time to break off this relationship. I'll be the bad guy. If he asks why, just say, 'My dad told me I could no longer talk to you.' And then I want you to promise me that you'll never talk to him again."

Dad had *never* made a request like this before. He had never forbidden me from seeing a certain boy or tried to run my life. On the contrary, he wanted all six of his children to grow up and become self-sufficient adults, even if that meant making a few mistakes along the way. But now he was inserting himself into a relationship that looked like it was heading to the altar. Though I was confused and unsure of what Dad learned about Randy, I felt betrayed and deceived about his true character. Then I remembered how we were always hiding our relationship at Pine Cove. I didn't like that, being secretive. It felt wrong.

"I promise I'll break it off, Dad."

And that's what I did the next time Randy called. After telling him that I never wanted to speak to him again, I hung up before he could reply.

Even though the split-up had to be done, I was heartbroken. This was a guy I thought I would marry one day. I had given part of my heart to him.

If I needed confirmation that Randy was a pathological liar, I received it a few days later when Jeff was visiting me in Nashville. My older brother had been my "protector" at City High School. If anyone wanted to date me, and Jeff didn't approve of them, he would threaten them by saying, "Don't you dare take my sister out." They had to go through Jeffrey Paul to get to me.

Not long after I told Jeff what happened, I received a phone call on my cellphone. I looked down at the phone number, which I didn't recognize. But I did recognize the Texas area code.

"I'm afraid it could be Randy," I said.

"Don't answer it," Jeff directed.

My brother waited two minutes, then hit "dial" on the missed call.

A smile came to Jeff's face. "Hey, is Randy there?" he asked in the friendliest voice he could muster.

"Yeah, just a second. Let me get him," said the voice.

When he came on the phone, he said, "Randy, this is Julianna's brother, Jeffrey. If you ever, ever attempt to call my sister again, I will come to Texas and personally beat you to a pulp."

That wasn't exactly turning the other cheek, but Randy never called again.

That phone call is what it took to realize that he really was a deceiver. I had asked Randy not to call me again, but he had used a friend's cell phone knowing that if he called on his phone, I'd recognize his number and not take the call.

My next phone call was to my father. "Dad, I'm so sorry. You were 100 percent right. I was mad at you for telling me not to talk to him anymore. I was convinced that he was okay, that it was just a misunderstanding. But now I know that you were right."

"Thanks, Jules. You know that I only want the best for you."

"I know, Dad. The only reason I listened to you is because I trust you so much. You never once led me astray when I was a young girl, so I knew I could trust you."

BEN

When I heard that I was going to room with Julianna's brother during summer league, I knew I would be spending a ton of time with him over the summer, and I didn't want things to be awkward between us. I just wanted to become friends with Jeff without him thinking I was trying to get to his sister. I never talked about Julianna unless he happened to bring her name up in a conversation.

Every Sunday, he would call Julianna or she would call him from Pine Cove. Sometimes she'd call early on Sunday morning, waking the both of us since he would be in the bed across the room from me.

I never asked to speak with her, although every once in a while, Jeff would say, "Julianna says hi!"

Even though she was on my mind, I did not e-mail her that summer. I hoped she would accompany her parents during their visits, but she never did. Her parents were really nice to me, always inviting me to join them for dinner at a nearby restaurant. As I got to know Jeff and Cheryl Gilmore—they insisted on me calling them by their first names—I thought, *This family is awesome. If things ever worked out with Julianna, this would be the greatest family to have as in-laws.*

Of course, it looked like things *weren't* going to work out with Julianna, and I reminded myself that I was okay with that.

A couple of hours before a game one night, in the Woodchucks' clubhouse, my manager, Steve Foster, and I were shooting the breeze about his playing days with the Cincinnati Reds as a relief pitcher. Fos had to retire after two seasons in the big leagues when he suffered one of the strangest career-ending injuries in the history of baseball. He wrecked his shoulder throwing baseballs at milk bottles on the *Tonight Show with Jay Leno* and never pitched in the majors again. I kid you not.

Fos was telling an amusing baseball anecdote when he stopped and looked at me. "You have a girlfriend?" he asked.

"No." It stung a bit to say that.

"Well, you better find one before you get to the big leagues."

Yeah, right. You really think I'm going to become a major league baseball player? "Why do you say that?" I asked.

"After you get there, you will never again know a girl's true intentions. It gets a lot harder to find what you are looking for once you're in the major leagues."

I appreciated how Fos was looking out for my welfare, but deep inside, I didn't see how it was possible to play major league baseball. I didn't even get drafted after my junior season, even after hitting over .400 and being named All-American. But hearing him say that I had the chops to play major league baseball boosted my confidence immeasurably. Fos obviously saw something in me as a player and believed that I had what it took to become a big league ballplayer—which is why he asked whether I had a girlfriend.

One night after a game, Jeff and I grabbed something to eat. We started swapping stories about our college ball experiences. Following his freshman year, Jeff had transferred from the University of Iowa to Dallas Baptist University because he wanted to pitch for a warm-weather team and place himself in a Christian college environment.

"DBU has a really good baseball program," Jeff said. "We're moving up to NCAA Division I next season, so we're going to play a lot of the Big 12 schools like Texas Tech and Oklahoma State. It's a big upgrade in competition for us."

"That's cool. I hope it works out—"

Jeff interrupted me. "Oh, and there's one more thing. We need a shortstop."

Shortstop? I was back to my old position with the Woodchucks and having a great summer. (I would lead the team in batting with a .319 average and be voted the team's most valuable player. We would also win the Northwoods League championship.)

Jeff leaned closer to make his best pitch. "Dude, you totally need to come to Dallas Baptist."

The wheels started turning in my mind. The higher level of competition in Division I would bolster my chances to play pro ball. I only had one year left, so if I was going to make a bold move like this, it was now or never.

"Tell me more about Dallas Baptist," I said.

Jeff said Dallas Baptist would be a great fit for me, give me a lot more exposure to major league scouts, and keep me in a Christian college environment. That all sounded great, but I was torn because transferring meant leaving Olivet, Coach Johnson, and all the great people I knew there. Coach Johnson had given me a chance to play college baseball when no one else wanted me.

Jeff put me in touch with Coach Mike Bard at Dallas Baptist, who told me that I had to get my release from Olivet Nazarene before he could offer me a scholarship. I sought my parents' counsel, and they saw nothing but upside. I lifted the matter up in prayer, asking the Lord if there was some reason I shouldn't transfer, that He'd make it apparent. Instead, I saw green lights. I wanted to play at the highest level I could to see if I could measure up.

Now it was a matter of asking Olivet Nazarene to release me from my scholarship so that I could transfer to DBU. When I spoke with Coach Johnson, he wasn't thrilled with the prospect of losing one of his star players, but in the end, he didn't want to stand in the way of my dreams of playing major league baseball.

You see, I loved the game of baseball, and I didn't want to stop playing.

JULIANNA

There was something else that Dad said after he asked me to break things off with Randy.

"You need to start dating Ben Zobrist," he said.

Dad had spent some quality time with Ben when he and Mom took in some games in Wisconsin, and he liked what he saw. The whole situation was comical: everyone in my family loved Ben Zobrist.

Not even one hour after I called Randy to break things off, I received an e-mail from Ben. *Hey, how are you doing?* he began. *Just thinking about you. We haven't talked in a really long time.*

I was blown away by the timing. I can't remember what I said in response to Ben, but I do remember starting to cry in my dorm room. When my roommate Lindsay Wells asked what was the matter, I showed her Ben's e-mail. "That's it," I said with resolve. "I'm praying from this day on that God will either put this guy in my life or take him out because I'm tired of this."

Little did I know that I would receive a lightning response from that prayer.

BEN

I sent that e-mail to Julianna as I was settling into Dallas Baptist. We had started fall ball, and I loved how things were shaping up. I wanted to know how good I really was, so this would be my opportunity to find out.

Two weeks later, I was hanging out with Jeff at his apartment. "Hey, I'm going up to Nashville to surprise Julianna for her birthday," he said. "Lance is coming with me. Do you want to come?" Lance Bina was one of our teammates.

Oh, no. This was getting to be too much for me. I had been thinking about this girl so much. I had been praying about her. I couldn't get Julianna out of my mind even though I hadn't seen her in more than a year. The last time we talked in person was following my summer league game with the Twin City Stars when we sat on a curb and chatted for two hours. I sent e-mails every now and then, but they were more of the "staying in touch" mode.

Of course, I couldn't say no to Jeff's idea. "When's her birthday?"

"Saturday, October 5," Jeff said. "We have a three-day weekend for fall break. Perfect timing."

"I would love to go . . . but—"

"Then what's the problem?"

"I gotta come clean with you. I've had feelings for Julianna for awhile, and I've been praying for the Lord to give me some sort of confirmation one way or another. If you can tell me there's nothing from her side, then I can just consider it closed. Do you know anything?"

There, it was out in the open. Cards on the table.

"She hasn't said anything to me, so I'll guess you'll just have to ask her."

I think Jeff enjoyed watching me squirm a bit.

"Don't worry about it," he continued. "Mom is flying in from Iowa, and there will be lots of people there. You'll fit right in. Besides, she won't know you're coming because she doesn't know I'm coming. It will be a surprise."

I remember driving away from his apartment feeling a sense from the Lord that He was finally giving me the opportunity to move forward in this part of my life, whether it was with Julianna or someone else. I was excited because I knew He was in control of the situation, but I was still nervous about what I might hear.

I'm going to talk to this girl and tell her that I have feelings for her. I have to know if she thinks we have a future.

Then again, she could blow me out of the water or kill me softly. I didn't foresee either of these options as a good thing, but then at least I'd know once and for all.

I made my upcoming visit a matter of prayer: *God, You're giving me the opportunity to put this to rest, if that's what You really want me to do. God, if You don't want me to have this girl, please take her out of my mind. Please don't let me think about her.*

That was proving to be impossible. Julianna Gilmore had taken up residence in my brain, and she was doing laps in my head.

JULIANNA

Ben didn't know it, but I was thinking about him a lot—and praying to the Lord every day that He would either bring Ben into my life or take him out.

Mom had come to Nashville for my birthday, and Lindsay's mom was in town, too. We decided to have a girls' day out so we went to the Mall of Green Hills outside downtown Nashville.

We were coming out of a clothing store when I heard some yahoos whistling at us from the second story balcony. I ignored them.

But Mom looked up. "Oh, those boys are cute," she said. That was very uncharacteristic of her. They whistled again.

I elbowed her. "Mom, don't look at them. That will only egg them on."

I kept walking, but Mom, Lindsay's mom, and Lindsay stopped in their tracks.

"What are you doing? Mom, you're the one who taught me never to look at boys when they're whistling at you."

"Oh, my goodness, Jules, just look."

I glanced up, and there was Jeffrey, Lance, and . . . *Ben?*

I sank to my knees in shock. I hadn't seen Ben in nearly sixteen months.

Here's how I described that event in my journal:

October 6, 2003

Oh, my goodness! Jeff surprised me yesterday and came to Nashville. He brought Lance and Ben with him. What can I say, Father, except that You are so good, and I praise You.

Tonight, at the end of the evening, Ben asked me if we could talk privately.

I said yes, but I was nervous. It was 12:30 a.m. when we started walking around the Belmont campus. It was a very nice night. Ben said he wanted to talk to me and be honest about his feelings. Boy, what a change for a guy.

He started from the beginning and told me about Dan and Liz telling him about me and giving him my e-mail address. Then he talked about us meeting a couple of times and how I decided I didn't want to talk to him anymore or for him to pursue me.

And Ben said he was fine all the time. He was at peace. But then we kept seeing each other randomly, and he said, "You were always in the back of my mind."

Ben told me he liked a girl this summer, but because of me, he couldn't pursue her. Jeff and Ben were roommates in Wisconsin, and when Ben asked Jeff what he thought of pursuing me, my brother said, "Sure."

This is so huge for me. Jeff told me this weekend that he called Mom and Dad to make sure they thought it was a good idea.

After Ben said all this, he said he just had to see if there was a possibility that something might or actually could happen, depending on my feelings. So I told him everything, from being annoyed by his e-mails to saying no, to desiring to hear from him, to seeing each other, to my short-lived relationship with Randy, to my frustration with my dad for pushing Ben on me, to now seeing him at my birthday party, just as I had prayed. He said, "Wow, I did not expect that answer. This is surreal, which I love."

We shared our ideas about serving the Lord, and we both got excited. Then he said he wanted to tell me what he'd be doing. He said he wanted to finish school, have a degree in communications, and then see if he gets drafted. If baseball doesn't work out, then something else will. It was adorable. He was telling me that he could take care of me.

Then he said, "If I feel like the Lord is leading us to be together, then I'll move to Nashville." Oh, wow! Talk about a guy who supports me. Thank you.

After talking more and more, he said he couldn't remember what I looked like before coming to Nashville. He remembered characteristics but not a picture. Then he said, And then I saw you at the mall . . . *he shook his head and didn't finish.*

Ben then said, "I don't look at you in the same way I've looked at other girls." Then he got the "look" in his eyes of wanting to kiss me, and my heart dropped. I thought, Great, *he's just like all the rest.*

But then Ben said, "I look at you, Julianna, and I just praise the Lord."

Who is this guy? Ben truly cares about me more than any other guy ever has.

You are good to me, Lord. Everything You've been teaching me, healing me from, to have someone who knowingly cares rather than flaunts me is amazing. I'm excited, but I'm so scared. Fear is not of You, so will You cast it out? Oh God, increase my care and my tenderness and affection. Thank You, Jesus, for Ben Zobrist, no matter how You use him in my life.

I wrote this at 2:00 a.m. in the morning, just minutes after I said goodbye to Ben for the evening. What a birthday!

BEN

I went back to where we were staying and pulled out my journal as well. Here is what I wrote at exactly the same time:

Dear Julianna:

I don't even know what to write to you right now. I just praise God, who is so amazing. I'm excited about how He is going to use us together. My heart is about to jump out of my chest right now onto the page because I know who you are! Yes, I do! I know it's crazy for me to be writing this right now when we still don't know each other real well, but after we talked tonight, I just couldn't believe what happened!

God is so amazing. There is no other way to explain it. How does He do things like this? It was like He had already told me and I wasn't ready to believe it until now. I never want us to forget about tonight. Always remember how I asked to talk to you in the back of Jeff's car and how he told me to be back by 12:30 when it was already 12:03.

Remember how I told you that I needed to get some things off my chest, and then I pretty much unloaded everything swirling around in my mind? Remember how I told you exactly what God was telling me about, even when I never saw you? How I kept thinking about you and didn't know why and how it was a God thing that kept bringing us closer and closer to each other until I couldn't deny thinking about you any more?

And then, remember how I told you that I needed to know if there was a possibility for us, or should I just put you out of my head for good? You'll never know how my heart leaped when you told me that the entire time you had been thinking about me, too, but not knowing why. And then how your story was so similar to mine.

Ah! God is awesome. How does He do that?

Jason just called, and I told him I was going to marry you someday. We've been talking about stuff like that since we were ten years old, so I figured I would be the first to let him know. He's my best friend. Oh, God is so awesome.

I'll never forget how we were walking by the side of your dorm when I told you God was calling me to live on the edge of heaven and earth. How He wanted me to be so consumed with bowing before His throne that I would be willing to give up all my hopes and dreams for this life and just worship Him at His feet, if that's what He wants me to do.

Remember the joy in my voice as we talked about that, and I'll never forget the look in your eyes when I was pouring out my heart to you. God is going to keep both of us accountable to living on the edge, willing to go wherever He wants us to go. We will always live on the edge.

Remember how we talked about both of our parents? My mom was unusually understanding when I said I needed to find out about you. Your dad always apparently knew that you were supposed to marry me. I'll remember how you said that he would always find a way to mention me and help you not forget about me.

Remember how earlier in our conversation we talked about feeling like God was trying to trick us, but God doesn't trick us. We must always remember that He makes the truth evident to us. Remember how after all this was said I didn't know what to

Even from the age of one, I loved tutus, baseball, and orange juice.

I'm two years old here, the age when my father put a plastic bat in my hands.

Pigtails and promises at age four: I was the happy-go-lucky kid who was always telling the family, "Let's laugh."

I'm a toddler here, having fun with my older sister Jessica.

I'm the classic middle child, the fourth oldest of six children. I'm checking out the family Christmas tree with my brother Jeff.

Like Julianna and every other little kid, I loved Christmas and always hoped for a new mitt or bat under the tree.

We did a lot of fun things as a family growing up, including visiting this strawberry patch. I'm the child with the pigtails.

Mom and Dad wanted to have a large family, so here we are in our Sunday best. I'm just to the left of Mom.

Dad was also my Little League coach growing up, and he was always encouraging me on the field.

I was a little squirt my freshman year of high school, one of the smallest kids in my class. I was just five feet, five inches and weighed 120 pounds—not exactly a power threat.

One of the highlights every summer was taking a family trip to St. Louis to see a Major League baseball game. We were big Cardinals fans growing up.

My senior year at Eureka High in the Midwest town of Eureka, Illinois. I had sprouted up to six feet, one inch, but I hadn't filled out yet.

Our first real date at the Reunion Tower in Dallas.

My nineteenth birthday party is where Ben surprised me and showed up in Nashville. I had been praying about him for two weeks, and we hadn't seen each other in almost two years. We all went to the Wild Horse Saloon to dance. We began dating that night.

This was my twentieth birthday party. My girlfriends bought me a new dress, took me to dinner, then dropped me off at the Melting Pot, where Ben surprised me and showed up. He told me he loved me that night.

After Ben and I started having a relationship on October 7, 2003, he sent me a rose one month later on November 7 to celebrate our "anniversary." Ben, ever the romantic, added a rose every month on the 7th until our one-year anniversary date.

It was at Christmastime shortly after we started dating that I shared a scarring experience with Ben that happened when I was twelve years old. He wrapped his arms around me and held me tight, which assured me of his love.

Here I'm hanging out with my roommates at Belmont University, Kari Kragness and Lindsay Wells.

Ben playing for Dallas Baptist University with my brother Jeff. I came down to visit and watch two of my favorite guys play ball!

The night Ben proposed to me, he bought this black velvet dress and asked me to wear it for a special dinner he had arranged at Percy Warner Park in Nashville, Tennessee.

Playing for the Salem Avalanche, a Class A affiliate of the Houston Astros (at the time).

During my second year in the minor leagues, I was engaged to Julianna and played shortstop for the Lexington Legends, a Class A affiliate of the Houston Astros.

I played well in Lexington, batting .304, and earned a mid-season promotion.

On the night before our wedding on December 17, 2005, we were both excited about the big day waiting for us.

We had to marry during baseball's offseason, so we had a white mid-December wedding in wintry Iowa.

After my father, Jeff Gilmore, walked me down the aisle
of the church he pastors, Parkview Church in Iowa City, Iowa,
Ben and his father, Tom, were waiting for me.

My father, Tom, performed
our wedding ceremony and
told those in attendance that
he had told me that girls
make your legs weak when I
was growing up, but that was
no longer true. "If you find
the right girl, she can make
you stronger," he said.

Photos courtesy of Sherry Pardee

Time to cut the cake
at the reception.

My family (top row, from left): Rosie, Jeffrey Paul, my father Jeff, and Jonathan; then Caroline, my mother Cheryl, and Liz.

I'm blessed with three sisters who are always there for me: (from the left) Caroline, Rosie, and Liz.

My family: Peter and my father Tom with (from the left) Jessica, my mother Cindi, Serena, and Noah.

Photos courtesy of Sherry Pardee

My parents always said if I made it to the major leagues, they'd be there for my debut. We were a happy bunch after my first game in a Rays uniform.

My dad always told me, "Jules, if you want the audience to bleed, you have to be hemorrhaging on stage."

Home improvement project! We bought our first home in Nashville after the 2007 season, and we've made the Nashville area our primary place of residence.

The *Say It Now* cover to my second CD.

My first red carpet experience happened in 2012 at the MovieGuide Faith & Values Gala near the heart of Hollywood. I did several on-camera interviews before I sang "Say It Now" during the show that was broadcast nationally on cable.

Several times I've had the privilege of singing the National Anthem before a Rays' game. The last occasion was during a 2013 playoff game against the Boston Red Sox.

I upped my power game during my breakout season in 2009, when I batted .297, smacked 27 home runs, and hit 28 doubles and 7 triples.

The Rays have had a lot to celebrate during my career, including a World Series appearance in 2008 and several runs in the playoffs.

I used to be a batter who took a lot of pitches, and while I'm still patient at the plate, I'll go after a pitch I like early in the count.

Sometimes I go old school with the socks.

I've always prided myself on my mitt work. My versatility in the field means that I can play right field, shortstop, and second base.

Photos courtesy of Skip Milos/Tampa Bay Rays

Making our own play-
ground in Phoenix during
the USA World Baseball
Classic.

During the 2013 All Star
game, I got to teach Zion
more about baseball.

USA World Baseball Classic

Driving with the top down is one of
our favorite things to do whenever
we go on dates.

Zion and Kruse are growing up around baseball. Here we are at the home run derby the day before the 2013 All-Star Game.

These are days that nap time is on a plastic stadium seat and Kruse's lullaby music is the sound of thousands of cheering fans.

Zion gets to join me in the clubhouse after games, which is one of his favorite things to do. Here we are before going into the clubhouse after making it into the 2013 postseason.

Zion and I at the 2013 All-Star Game in New York. Ben was picked as the lone Rays' representative.

We both agree that we're blessed with a growing family, my baseball
career, and Julianna's music. We'll see where the Lord takes us.

Our family: Kruse, Julianna, Ben, and Zion.

say next. Remember how we stood outside your dorm and I told you, "When I just look at you, I praise God."

Remember that. I will always do that . . . always.

I'll never forget seeing that statement settle into your eyes and then how I continued to compliment you until I had to say goodnight before I ruined the moment. It was an amazing conversation and we will never forget it because it was the night that God made us finally come together and unite in spirit. We knew deep down before but now I know and God has given me solid evidence and proof to me that you are the girl I've been dreaming and praying about.

Let's praise Him together for His great and mighty and awesome plans. He is great and greatly to be praised. We will trust Him with our lives and we will love Him with all that we have while we love each other.

I love you already, but I probably won't tell you that for a while.

Ben

I read those words today, ten years later, and think, *That is so cheesy, man.* But reading my thoughts is like holding up a snapshot. I was in the moment, and that's what I felt.

I was sure that I had found the girl I wanted to marry.

But first, both of us needed to find out if this was really going to work out.

A PITCH OVER
THE MIDDLE

JULIANNA

On a Sunday morning in a Belmont student parking lot, Ben gave me a warm but brief hug before he departed for Dallas with Jeff and Lance. Then he pulled me aside so that the others were out of earshot.

"I'm looking forward to what happens between us, but if it's okay with you, let's talk every three or four days on the phone. When we talk, I want our conversations to have purpose and meaning. I don't want to chat so often that we lose that purpose."

This was a welcome change. "I like your idea," I said.

Up to this point, I was used to guys calling me every day when I was dating them. It was obvious that they were needy and clingy. I loved the fact that Ben didn't yearn to talk to me every day. I appreciated the leadership and forethought he put into this.

However, I wasn't so sure I liked this idea when Ben didn't call me for *five* whole days. I was getting antsy to hear from him. I had been used to past relationships where I could dictate the pace of how quickly things moved, and this was a first test of submitting and trusting in Ben's leadership.

When he finally called, one of the first things he asked was if he could take me out on an "official" date.

"Sure, but you're in Dallas and I'm in Nashville, remember?" I laughed.

BEN

I was fully aware that there was 664 miles separating us. I wanted to see her, but I also didn't want to rush things.

Before calling her regularly and asking her out, I phoned her father to formally inform him about my intentions to pursue a relationship with Julianna because my dad had always made prospective guys do an interview with him before they took out my sisters. In my situation, Jeff thanked me for the courtesy call and wished me all the best.

After asking Julianna out and her reminding me that she was in Nashville—which I knew, of course—I asked if she could find someone who could come to Dallas with her.

"Let me ask around," she said.

JULIANNA

My roommate, Lindsay Wells, couldn't make it, but Lindsey Jones, who was across the hall from me and had become a good friend, said she was up for an adventure, which is what our trip turned out to be.

Three weeks later, on Friday, October 31, 2003—Halloween—
we departed Nashville at daybreak in my well-worn Mercury
Villager, a hand-me-down minivan with plenty of carpooling
miles on it. Our MapQuest directions said it would take nine hours
and forty-three minutes to get to Dallas, but I'm afraid it took a lot
longer to arrive at Dallas Baptist.

Here's what happened. I drove while Lindsey played naviga-
tor. It was pretty much a straight shot westbound on Interstate
40 until we made a southwesterly jog onto Interstate 30. At four
o'clock in the afternoon, we were inside the Dallas metro area. We
exited Loop 7, as per MapQuest's instructions. Suddenly, we were
in a sketchy part of town. Lindsey and I looked at each other. This
wasn't where we were supposed to be.

We kept going, thinking we'd eventually see the right street
and make a right turn that would take us to Dallas Baptist. We
must have driven six or eight miles looking for that blasted street.
We had left the commercial zone and were motoring through a
run-down residential area.

"This is not right," I said. "I think we have to turn around and
go back."

"Great idea." Lindsey then locked her door, and I followed suit.

While I was figuring out a way to turn around, I saw a tan
car—a low-rider—slow down in front of us. There were four guys
in the car. Two in the front and two in the back.

Suddenly, a serious-looking dude in the backseat opened up his
passenger window. He hung his body out of the car and stared at
us. Then he flashed a smile filled with gold teeth.

I held my breath, and Lindsey shuttered. "I'm getting afraid,"
she said.

Fear caused me to grip the steering wheel tighter. "What do
you think I should—"

Before I could finish my sentence, he pointed his right hand at us with his index finger and thumb extended in the form of a gun. He took aim and pretended to shoot us.

I freaked out and slammed on the brakes. Fortunately, no one was behind us in two lanes of traffic.

"Turn around!" Lindsey screamed. "We have to get out of here!"

I cranked the steering wheel to the left. My minivan hit the median curb, but I didn't care about my alignment. I bolted across the median, completed an impromptu—and illegal—U-turn, and peeled down the boulevard as fast as I could go. I looked in the rearview mirror. They weren't following, but I had a good fright on Halloween.

I breathed a sigh of relief and reached for my cell phone. Ben answered immediately, but I figured it wasn't a good idea to call a boyfriend you barely know when you don't know where you are and you're panicking. He sounded like the voice of reason, though, advising us to work our way back to the interstate so that we could figure out where we were. We followed his instructions and discovered that we had gotten off on Loop 6. We should have gone one more exit to Loop 7.

When we arrived at Dallas Baptist, Ben and a few other guys were in Jeffrey Paul's apartment, where Lindsey and I would also be staying for the weekend. We walked in with our sleeping bags and luggage, tremendously excited that we had arrived. Hugs were exchanged. Lindsey also brought her guitar, so it wasn't long before the guys were saying, *We want to hear y'all sing.*

Lindsey and I obliged them with a Patty Griffin number because you could really belt on those, plus we were in Dallas and her songs were rooted in Texas-style country. When it came to making plans for the evening, the guys already had things mapped out: we would go out to dinner and then head over to Billy Bob's, a Texas saloon-type-of-place where we could go line dancing.

That sounded like fun. I slipped into a purple country western outfit with a real tight tan skirt that was cut short on the left leg, long on the right. I wore a purple button-up blouse with lace on the shoulders. I thought I looked cute. Then Ben stepped out of a bedroom wearing a pearl-snap shirt tucked into his blue jeans with a belt buckle the size of a Subway sandwich. He topped off the silly-looking outfit with a Stetson cowboy hat and cowboy boots. The only thing missing were spurs.

BEN

I was trying to be funny, but I guess Julianna wasn't impressed with my humor.

JULIANNA

He looked like a total dud—like a baseball player trying to imitate a country artist. My mood changed as rapidly as a tornado funnel whipping across the Texas plains. *I don't want to date him anymore. I think I'm over this.*

We hadn't even gone out on a real date and I was mentally packing it in. Usually my relationships lasted two months. It looked like this one was going to last two days.

When we arrived at Billy Bob's with a live country band, Ben asked me to dance, and even though I'm a dancing fool, I didn't want to line dance with him. After a few songs, Ben tried again. I reluctantly said yes and made a half-hearted attempt to do a two-step with him, but right off I could see that he had two left feet when it came to line dancing. There was no timing or rhythm.

That was another turnoff. I was used to being in dance classes at Belmont with guys who really knew what they were doing. Ben was clearly out of his element.

BEN

I'll admit that Julianna threw me for a loop on the dance floor. Something was bothering her, but I didn't know what it was. I figured that she was in a new environment and needed time to sort things out.

"Are you doing okay?" I tried to match her steps for the Electric Slide dance.

She shrugged her shoulders and kept moving her feet. Her body language was saying, *I don't want to be here.*

I was bummed she felt that way. Maybe this whole relationship thing wasn't meant to be after all, but that's what this weekend was all about. We would be going on our first official date the following night, and if she was still acting withdrawn, then we would have to talk about what changed.

Until our first dinner date, I tried to make the best of an awkward situation.

JULIANNA

For a completely prideful, self-consumed college-age girl, I was torn. On one hand, I didn't really want to be with Ben that evening. On the other hand, though, I definitely wanted to be with him that weekend. I think I was treating him like a jerk just to see what he would do. It's awful to admit that years later, but I think that's what happened.

How did he handle my petulance? He exuded grace. He showed patience. He still tried to talk to me like everything was okay. That Friday night, I didn't know a more accommodating or understanding man in the world.

I think I was standoffish because we both thought that we were *supposed* to be in a relationship with each other. The truth of the matter is that I was thinking I was pretty hot stuff and not really sure I was into this guy. But there was another issue in play, and it was that I was afraid of falling in love. I was afraid of disappointment. I was afraid of getting hurt again.

In my mind, I was comparing Ben to my father and my brothers, because they set the standard for me—and that was a high bar. Then my mind would remind me that I didn't want to be with my dad or my brothers the rest of my life because I wanted a life of my own.

You can see the push-pull going on in my brain. Over the last few weeks, I had gotten used to speaking to Ben over the phone and felt comfortable with him, although we put a limit on the number of phone conversations. We enjoyed flirting and joking with each other over the phone, but when I saw him in person in Dallas, a completely different dynamic took center stage.

A lot would be decided during our first official date the following night.

BEN

I had decided before Julianna left Nashville that I was going to go all out to make our first date something we'd never forget. I chose the Reunion Tower in downtown Dallas, a spectacular fifty-five-story observation tower topped with a geodesic dome formed with aluminum struts. Inside the glowing glass ball was a revolving restaurant offering 360-degree views of the Dallas skyline and the surrounding metropolis.

We took a long elevator ride to the Antares restaurant, where a hostess confirmed my reservation and seated us at a two-person table right next to a window. I wanted to impress Julianna, and that's what happened. As darkness fell on Dallas, her face lit up as she took in the amazing view of city streets and the purple-and-orange sky that surrounded us.

JULIANNA

I'll admit that up to this point, I had been standoffish to Ben. The whole situation scared me because I was just waiting for that moment of failure on his part. I knew I was being overly critical—like how he dressed in cowboy clothes and looked silly line dancing—but I was making up all these things in my head as an excuse to push him away at some point.

On the other hand, my emotions were conflicted because I sensed that once Ben and I started dating, then he would become my husband. I'm not sure why I felt that way since we had only spent five hours of time alone before this weekend, but I did sense that God was orchestrating something about Ben Zobrist and was clearly placing him into my life for a reason. So even though there was a lot riding on this evening, I was open to whatever happened because I had prayed that God would make it clear whether Ben was the person He had waiting for me.

The Antares was certainly the fanciest restaurant I'd ever been in. Everything about it was cool—the décor, the floor-to-ceiling windows, and the way the floor slowly revolved on its axis.

We sat down, placed the white linen napkins on our laps, and opened up our leather-bound menus. Remember, this was back in 2003, more than a decade ago, but the cheapest thing on the menu was a vegetarian plate for $27, and that didn't include a green salad, which was another ten bucks. The New York strip was well beyond $50.

I asked for a petite filet, one of the cheaper entrées at $32, because I love steak. Ben ordered a pasta dish with shrimp, lobster, and other delicacies from the ocean. I knew this was a lot of money for a college student, but Ben was insistent that he treat me special. We saved money by not ordering wine, which wasn't going to happen anyway for two reasons: I was underage at nineteen years old, and Ben had never had any alcohol—wine, beer, or cocktails—in his life. His family believed drinking was wrong, he explained, so he had never even tried beer or wine growing up.

I didn't drink at all in high school either and certainly didn't party at Belmont, but I had grown up with parents who felt that a glass of wine accompanying a fine meal wasn't a big deal. There were family occasions, like Thanksgiving or Christmas dinner, where they let me have a sip or two of red wine. But drinking never appealed to me as I was growing up.

Wine or no wine, we had a wonderful evening. Conversation flowed easily, and I relaxed. When our entrées arrived with a flourish, we dug into the most delicious food.

"Do you want to try one of my shrimp?" Ben asked.

"Yeah, sure. That would be great."

He slipped his fork under an elongated crustacean and then placed the cooked shrimp and some sauce on the edge of my plate. That was one big shrimp from the Gulf of Mexico. I wasn't sure how to eat the thing. I attempted to stab it with my fork only to watch in horror as the jumbo shrimp shot across the room and landed underneath the plate of an Asian woman eating with her husband.

I fully expected the older woman to look up and wonder why the sky was suddenly raining shrimp, *but she didn't notice.* Her husband was clueless as well.

Ben and I looked at each other, and for a long moment, we did our best to stop ourselves from busting out laughing. Then we couldn't hold the dam back, and we let out a gentle burst of smirks and laughs.

We didn't say anything because we didn't have to—nor did we dare make eye contact with the nearby couple. This was our own little secret. I loved that he laughed with me and not *at* me. From that moment, our conversation flowed like water traveling down a fast-moving stream.

BEN

After dinner, I drove us back to the DBU campus and swung by a special spot where I liked to pray on occasion. I showed her the place, and then we prayed that our relationship would be honoring to God.

Next we swung by the baseball diamond. It wasn't too late, maybe 10:30 or so. The moonlit evening had a soft air to it.

We parked behind the outfield near a gate that I had propped open that afternoon. I led her toward the field, carrying a blanket and a boom box.

"Where are we going?" Julianna asked.

"You'll see."

I led her through the gate and toward the pitcher's mound. I set down the blanket on the grass behind home plate and turned on some music. After talking awhile, I thought we'd give the dancing thing a try again.

JULIANNA

When Ben asked me if I wanted to dance, I said I'd love to. Everyone deserves a second chance.

Ben pushed play on the boom box, and then he outstretched his arms to dance. I accepted his embrace, and we started slow dancing to just about the worst un-danceable Christian music I'd ever heard.

First, the cowboy garb on Friday night, and now I was slow-dancing to schmaltzy Christian music under the stars. In baseball terms, this was two strikes against him, so he was way behind in the count. But I continued to give him grace and didn't want him to strike out.

I reminded myself that I had been raised by a very mature mother who never understood Dad's warped sense of humor. They've been married a billion years, but she still didn't get his jokes. She still laughed anyway. What I'm trying to say is that I never expected a fairy tale and knew too much about life to expect one. My struggle lay in considering myself smarter than or superior to him.

BEN

Yeah, I was a total nerd and a hopeless romantic. Some of that was good, but now that I look back, I think I was trying too hard to make things perfect.

JULIANNA

Mercifully, his choice of music got better. A couple of quiet danceable country songs came on, and we held each other close—but not *real* close—and danced for another twenty minutes or so.

We packed up the boom box. Waiting for us in Jeff's dorm room was Lindsey and a few others who were hanging out.

Lindsey and I hit the road right after breakfast Sunday morning since we couldn't miss Monday classes. As miles of interstate passed by, I had plenty of time to think about Ben, who showed me that he had an ideal way that he saw the relationship going. It was apparent that he loved the Lord and just wanted to be where God wanted him to be. He didn't care where that was or what he would do. He wasn't worried about being comfortable or about being poor. His goal was to be right where God wanted him.

That evening, I saw a lot that I liked about Ben—his spiritual leadership, his sense of knowing that he was going somewhere, and the fact that he clearly adored me. He didn't say this at the Reunion Tower, but in so many words here's what I heard:

God's taking me places, and I don't know where that is yet, but I'd love to have you come along as my partner in this thing called life.

BEN

Quite simply, I did all those things in Dallas because that's what a godly Christian man does to sweep a girl off her feet, but what I realize now is that I was doing those things to impress her and prove that I could be everything Julianna needed me to be. I would later find out how wrong I was.

Even though there were a couple of bumpy moments, I thought our first weekend together went very well, which was confirmed in subsequent phone conversations between Dallas and Nashville. One of those discussions that sticks in my mind was when I made known my intention not to kiss her until we were engaged. "That would be the right thing to do," I declared. "That's if we get engaged, of course."

I wanted Julianna to know that I wasn't jumping to any conclusions or taking anything for granted regarding marriage, but until then, kissing or doing anything physical between us was off the drawing board.

JULIANNA

When Ben said that over the phone, I was deeply impressed, especially after some of my previous interactions with the opposite sex, including those who wanted more than a kiss.

BEN

The DBU baseball team had 6:00 a.m. workouts during the fall. A few weeks after Julianna returned to Nashville, I sat in the bleachers and wrote about our first date in my journal:

> *God has and is still solidifying my purpose as a man, and I think He is calling us—me and you—to something special. I know this because I feel the forces of evil tremble when I think about our future together. God is calling us to live lives worthy of His calling, and I want you to know that I can't do that as well without you.*
>
> *Satan knows how magnificently God will be able to use two hearts like ours that have been unified into one. And God wants me to be the leader of us to protect you and love you and sacrifice for you, and to treat you like Christ is treating the church. I promise that I will love you and serve you and sacrifice myself for you.*
>
> *God is answering my prayers, and I do understand how amazingly He has made you. I have the great and blessed responsibility of encouraging you to be the woman that He has made you to be. Another thing God has been teaching me more and more is to crave the Word. It is the truth and the only thing that we can stand on. We must always go back to the Word whenever there is a question that's too great.*
>
> *Whenever we are struggling, we must fall on the promises of God that are founded in the Word. That is where our strength must always come from. I need you to remind me of it when I am*

struggling, and I promise to always lift you up by it when you are struggling. I need Joshua 1:5. I need to hear Jeremiah 29:11–13. I need to be reminded of Galatians 2:20. This is where our hope and strength must be built upon. His Word must be our lifeline, and it will endure forever.

I love to hear your voice. I save the messages you leave on my phone so I can hear your voice whenever I want. You bring joy to my heart and a smile to my face. Could we have had a better first date a couple of weeks ago? In your letter to me last week, you wrote that it was magical, and you were so right. Stuff like that only happens in fairy tales, but I guess that is what happens when you let God write your love story.

When I held you behind home plate and danced with you, I was dancing with the woman of my dreams. The beauty of your eyes are unmatched to me.

Earlier in the night we prayed together for the first time, and I held your hands. We linked our hearts in another way. Yes, our time alone with the Lord is very important, but we need to continue to make prayer together one of our highest priorities. After all, God answers prayers to those who abide in Him.

By the way, I loved playing baseball with you earlier that day. That was so much fun. You setting the ball up on the tee for me—I am sure we'll have more fun with that stuff in the future. The greatest part of the weekend, though, was on the way back from Billy Bob's. It was really late. We were sitting in the middle and my arm was on the back of the seat. You fell asleep, and I just watched you. You looked like an angel.

Your head started to fall slowly until it rested on my shoulder. At that moment, I don't know if there was a happier person on the planet than me. I felt like a king. I had an angel on my shoulder, and it was you. It was one of those moments that seems unimportant, but one that I will always cherish.

You are so beautiful, and believe me you can fall on my shoul-
der any time! That is the one time I enjoy my arm falling asleep
and being all tingly. I love you already, but it's more than a feel-
ing. I am committed to you, and that is God's plan. He brought
us together. No wonder I am falling so fast and hard for you.

With love,

Ben

I know—another mound of cheeseball. I'm having a hard time
reading this too! I sound like a girl.

JULIANNA

We can laugh about it now, but you can see how we were beginning
to give our hearts to each other. I was starting to love this man,
which meant I was starting to trust Ben.

As the trust grew, I began to have this burning feeling in my
gut that I needed to tell him something. I needed to tell him what
happened to me at age twelve.

Here's what I wrote in my journal in early December 2003:

My heart is hiding for fear of pain, even though the one
knocking is one that I've come to love.

If I show you the scar, will you turn away?

Will you walk back to my past and see the shame that is eat-
ing me or will tears of love wash over my soul and the warmth
of your caress bring life back to me?

My love, please don't let it hurt you. My Maker has made
this bleeding heart a scar. Will you help me carry it? I need to
know if you will. Please don't hide for if you do, my heart will
drop and my scar will bleed again.

Oh God, must I really show him?

STEPPING UP TO
THE PLATE

BEN

Now that we were officially a couple, I couldn't make plans to see Julianna again fast enough. Our next opportunity to spend some time together would be during Christmas break.

Normally, it's a three-hour drive from Eureka to Iowa, but this being the depth of winter, I was slowed down by icy conditions as I traveled past snow-covered cornfields and barren trees. The Gilmore family couldn't have been more welcoming upon my arrival, and I bunked with Jeffrey Paul in his bedroom.

On Sunday morning, we went to Parkview Church, where I heard her father preach for the first time. Jeff was similar to Dad in that they both preached out of the Bible, but they shepherded different-sized churches. Parkview had a congregation of a thousand with three Sunday morning services, while Liberty Bible was a small church on the edge of a small town with two hundred members and one Sunday morning service.

The highlight for me was hearing Julianna sing for the first time behind a worship band and all miked up. She performed a solo of "Mary Sweet Mary" with the most beautiful voice.

I sat upfront on the left side of the auditorium thinking about how cool it was that I was dating this girl who sang about Jesus with such an amazing voice. She seemed to have a special ability to not only bring notes out of her mouth but connect with the audience as well. She made performing look easy, which was a gift similar to my world, where great ballplayers always made the game look easy.

Then another thought came to mind: *If our relationship goes forward, she has to share her beautiful voice with as many people as she can.*

JULIANNA

I loved having Ben with me during the holidays. He fit right into our family, and I could see that everyone approved of the match.

I knew I was going to marry him. And since I was going to marry him, he needed to know about my past—a past that included a secret burning a hole in my heart. The memory of that awful attack was always in the room, much like a photograph hanging on a wall. All I had to do was glance in that direction, and recollections flooded my subconsciousness.

During the week that Ben stayed with us, we stayed up and talked after everyone else had gone to bed. Some nights, we chatted until 3 o'clock in the morning. (One time we heard my dad's alarm clock go off as we were talking in the living room. We raced to our bedrooms because that meant it was 4:30 a.m.)

On this particular evening, long after midnight, we were laying on our bellies, propped up on our elbows, talking and watching the golden flames dance in our gas-burning fireplace. The setting was peaceful as we laid on the carpeted floor next to the Christmas tree, laced with white lights and our favorite ornaments, many of them containing great meaning.

My heart was pounding because I knew it was time to share my secret. Knowing that we had come to this moment made me became extremely nervous, but I was cognizant that this was the time to tell Ben something about my background.

I straightened up and sat cross-legged on the soft carpet. Then I reached behind my head and loosened the band holding my ponytail in place. I let my shoulder-length hair fall over my face. I didn't want Ben to see me when I revealed the secret. I wanted to hide.

"I need to tell you something. Will you sit next to me?"

Ben brought himself up and drew closer to me as he crossed his legs and sat next to me. I could see the look of concern. He sensed something was in the air.

"Can you please hold my hand?" I asked.

"Are you okay?" Ben took my right hand into his. "What's wrong?"

I couldn't look at him. I looked down, my hair covering my face. "Something happened to me when I was twelve years old."

I hesitated because I knew I was about to plunge into an area of darkness.

"I was molested."

I looked up and saw Ben's face, which looked drawn and sad and mad—all at the same time. I had never seen him look so serious.

"What happened?" Ben remained calm. There was no outburst on his part.

"I was at a church camp that summer with my friend Christy. We were running late for the evening session just as it was getting dark. We were walking from our cabin to the meeting hall when we heard six guys yelling stuff at us from the woods.

"We ignored them and kept walking. Once we sat down in the meeting hall, Christy and I realized that we forgot our Bibles, so we went back to our cabins to get them. Then we heard some pounding on the walls, which scared us. Then the pounding stopped and we heard voices leaving. We waited until we thought it was safe, probably five minutes or so. We snuck out of the cabin and started walking because we didn't want to be late for chapel."

Tears were forming in my eyes because I was coming to the hard part. Ben maintained a stoic expression and nodded for me to continue.

"The next thing I knew, these six guys came out of nowhere. Christy ran for it and escaped, but they surrounded me, making nasty comments."

"How old were they?" Ben asked.

"I don't know. Probably sixteen or seventeen. They looked like high school students. They were definitely bigger and stronger than me."

"So what happened next?"

"The leader was a fat guy with kind of a mohawk. He was the first to rush me, and the others followed. They pushed me to the ground and grabbed at my clothing and . . . ." I couldn't finish.

"Did they—?"

"No, I wasn't raped. But I kept trying to fight off the guy on top of me. I got a hold of his T-shirt and ripped off a huge chunk, which really pissed him off. Next thing I knew, they were making a run for it. They must have figured someone would see them because they started running into the woods."

I then told Ben how dirty I felt afterward—inward and outward—and how I tried to wash up. "Christy came back with our youth pastor and found me in the girls' bathroom. I was really shook up. I told him I was okay and that nothing had happened, but I lied."

"Did anyone call the authorities?"

"I told the youth pastor that I didn't want to make a scene, but I was in a certain amount of shock, so I hid what actually happened. Afterward, I had nightmares and wondered, *Did I make this all up in my head?* I wanted to believe so much that this didn't happen."

A flood of tears were released as I remembered the shame and humiliation I felt from what those mean boys did to me. Then another thought hit me: *Am I pure enough for Ben? Would hearing my story cause him to leave me?*

I didn't give voice to those questions, but Ben sensed my thoughts. He wrapped his arms around me and held me tight. He didn't say anything for the longest time.

Then he pulled back with the most kind expression on his face and gazed into my tear-soaked eyes. "Jules, that is not who you are anymore," he said.

Ben's simple, declarative sentence stunned me. He was right. I wasn't that little girl any more. As much as that horrendous event had stayed with me, lurking below the surface, I didn't have to let it define who I was.

What Ben said that evening started the process of freeing myself from memories of that attack. I was assured that Ben's love for me would not diminish one iota.

In fact, he made me feel even more loved *because* of my story. In the years to come, Ben would help me realize that the most powerful thing I could do was to acknowledge what had happened to me on that terrible twilight evening.

BEN

When I heard Julianna painstakingly relive those horrific moments, my first reaction was that we needed to track down those guys and bring them to justice, but I quickly dismissed that thought because too much time had passed. What Julianna needed at that moment was to feel safe with me. That's why I drew her close and said, "I will always be there for you. I will always protect you."

That moment of sharing was a crucial time in our relationship. Up until then, she had always been upbeat and rarely, if ever, shown fear in a situation—unless she was lost in a bad section of Dallas. She expected the best and assumed the best from others. But this was an event in her life where I could see the apprehension within her heart. She was clearly struggling, but I wasn't sure what to say.

JULIANNA

What I liked is that Ben didn't offer any clichés—*I know how you're feeling* or *We'll get through this*. He didn't try to counsel me either. What happened between us that evening was literally the start of the conversation and the end of the conversation.

I breathed a heavy sigh of relief, and my love for Ben Zobrist grew. His patience and wisdom amazed me.

A couple of nights later, we were hanging out on the living room couch again, late at night. Everyone else had gone to bed. We had just finished watching a movie called *Napoleon Dynamite* and laughed our heads off. In case you haven't seen it, it's a movie about a slacker high school student from a small Idaho town who deals with his bizarre family life. There were some great lines in the film, like "He's out to prove he's got nothing to prove."

Ben started mimicking some of the other memorable lines, like *I love the way your sandy hair floats in the air.* And then he touched my head in a playful way, which was a form of intimacy.

There we were, sitting next to each other, feeling close. I don't care what he said about not kissing me until we got engaged, I wanted to kiss him! That was the only thing in my brain at that time. What was taking him so long?

I scooted closer. He scooted a little further from me. I scooted a little bit closer. He moved again. At some point, he figured out what I was doing. He was also running out of couch. When I had him totally pinned against the end of the sofa, I leaned in. I was practically puckering my lips.

Still, he held back.

So I kissed him. Finally.

Then he returned the kiss. In a very big way.

We laughed as I drew away. "Hey, you said you weren't going to kiss me until we got engaged!" I teased.

Ben knew he had been had. "I knew it was pointless to resist."

BEN

These days, I can tease Julianna about playing the role of Delilah to my Samson, but I would have waited until our engagement until she forced herself upon me. I think. But we stopped at first base, to use a baseball term.

I rounded first base a lot more times in Dallas—I mean, on the ball field. Everything I hoped that transferring to Dallas Baptist would be—the upgrade in competition, the proximity to pro scouts, and the chance to raise my game—came to fruition.

I led the team in hitting with a .389 average, collected 15 doubles, and knocked in 64 RBIs. I anchored the infield at shortstop and was named to the National Christian College Athletic

Association (NCCAA) All-American team. We finished with a regular season record of 40–16 and beat a lot of quality teams from schools ten times our size—like the University of Oklahoma. Jeff Gilmore, my future brother-in-law—oops, I'm getting ahead of myself—was the ace of the pitching staff, compiling a 10–3 record with a 2.96 ERA. A team highlight was winning the 2004 National Christian College Athletic Association's Baseball World Series in Celina, Ohio.

I hoped I was good enough to get picked in the June draft—and was thrilled when the Houston Astros made me their sixth-round pick. I was home in Eureka when I heard the good news, and every Zobrist in the state of Illinois was excited about my chance to play professional baseball. No one from Eureka had ever played in the minor leagues or major leagues before, so it was quite an honor. It was like God was saying, *Look what I can do if you commit your work to Me and you follow Me where I want you to go. I can do things that you don't think are even possible.*

When the Astros organization called, they told me to report to the Tri-City ValleyCats in the New York-Pennsylvania League (NYPL). This was a Class A rookie league, the bottom rung of the ladder. I had nowhere else to go but up.

My parents threw me a going-away party and filled the house with family, friends, and old coaches. After everyone had left, Dad and I found ourselves in my old bedroom—a bedroom filled with memories of the best childhood any kid could have.

"Dad, the way I look at things, I'm a baseball-playing missionary. But I don't have to raise support like I did for Mexico. Instead, I'm going to reach people for Christ, whether it's my teammates, fans, or whatever."

Dad looked intensely at me. "Here's what is important to me. I don't care what you do for a living as long as you live for God."

Dad always had the right words to say.

The ValleyCats played an abbreviated 68-game "short season" in the upstate New York town of Troy, just outside of Albany. I led the fourteen-team league in hitting with a .339 average, which raised some eyebrows in the Astros' front office. I was told I would be going to the Instructional League in Florida after the minor league season was over so I could work on my game.

Julianna and I continued to get along famously, even though this was proving to be a long-distance relationship. While I was in New York, she sent me a card with these words:

> *Ben,*
>
> *I got this card the day we found out you were drafted. I want you to know that you rock my world. Not only because you are a professional baseball player, but because of every-thing you are.*
>
> *I love your passion for the game, even if I don't know what Cooperstown is. I love how you work so hard. I love that you can't take compliments very well. I love that you know you can always be better. I love that you are excited to con-tinue to let God use you through your life and playing the game. I appreciate so much how you have let me be a part of this.*
>
> *You amaze me,*
>
> *Julianna*

JULIANNA

We spoke on the phone while he was playing baseball in Florida— much more often than once every three or four days. Try every day.

We teased each other that our "one-year anniversary" was coming up—the night of my birthday when we walked around the Belmont campus after midnight and declared our feelings for one another.

But I wasn't going to see him for my twentieth birthday. He was still playing in the Instructional League and called me that morning to wish me a happy birthday. I was starting my junior year at Belmont.

My birthday, October 5, fell on a Tuesday, but that wasn't going to stop me and my girlfriends from having some fun. Ten girlfriends took me out to dinner and gave me a wonderful present: a maroon red silk dress, cut symmetrically in a V-neck style. They had all pitched in and bought it at a boutique called Posh.

The plan after dinner was to take in a music performance somewhere along Music Row in downtown Nashville. We were all dressed up and looked so cute as we walked up and down Broadway.

After the show, someone piped up, "Let's go get dessert!"

"Yeah, at the Melting Pot!" chimed in another friend. "They have the best chocolate fondue."

I loved hanging out with my girlfriends. They were always up for spontaneous fun. When we walked into the Melting Pot restaurant, I followed the pack toward the back of the restaurant. Everyone sure seemed to be in a good mood, and several of my girlfriends glanced back and smiled at me.

We rounded a corner, and there in a two-person booth sat Ben with a rose in his hand.

I put my hands on my face. "What are you doing here?"

"I flew in from Orlando. Sorry I couldn't be here sooner. Looks like your girlfriends can keep a secret." Ben nodded toward the well-dressed young ladies surrounding us.

"They sure can!" Oh, yeah, my girlfriends were in on it.

Ben looked amazing. He even had a rose on the table for me.

I heard some coughing, and then my girlfriends waved good-bye and were gone.

We ordered a chocolate fondue with cut-up bananas, straw-berries, and angel food cake. As we dipped the morsels into the heavenly melted chocolate, Ben told me about all the hoops he had to jump through to make it to Nashville. "And I have to leave early in the morning to get back to the team," he said.

"Thanks for making my birthday special," I said.

We left the Melting Pot and headed over to Centennial Park in the west end of Nashville. We were walking around, holding hands, when we sat down on a bench underneath a tree. There was a sliver of moon that night, so it was pretty dark next to a water pond. We were just talking, when Ben said, "I didn't want to tell you this so early, but I love you."

I froze.

He waited.

And waited.

I knew in my head that after he said those three simple yet evoking words that I didn't want to say *I love you* back if I didn't mean it. I took my time thinking this through. I knew I cared for Ben more than anyone I had cared for before. I knew he treated me way better than any guy had before him. He knew me better than anyone else, but those three words were freighted in weight. This was a crossing-the-Rubicon moment in our relationship. You can't take those words back.

Ben leaned closer. "Please say something."

To me, Ben might as well have proposed. When I was younger, I had written various poems about how I wouldn't tell anyone I loved him until he was actually my husband, similar to Ben telling himself that he would never kiss a girl until he was engaged.

But that was an ideal, an abstract. Now I was dealing with a reality—the man I knew I was going to marry had just told me that he loved me for the first time.

I knew I was making him nervous, taking so long to respond. But I wanted to check my heart and be sure that I had fallen in love with Ben Zobrist.

I had.

"I love you, too," I said. There, I was brave enough to utter that simple sentence.

Soon, we were saying "I love you" on the phone when we finished our calls. Not every time, but on the occasions it made sense.

And then Ben *showed* me that he loved me. When the Instructional League was over, he moved to Nashville and lived with a Christian guy named Phil Carpenter. It would only be for a few months, but we would be together, living in the same city for the first time.

BEN

I told Julianna that I was willing to live in Nashville during the off-season to support her musical aspirations. Then in February 2005, my older sister, Jessica, and younger brother, Pete, came to visit me—their first time in Nashville. We had to show them all the tourist sights, like the Opryland Hotel, where you expect to pass country belles with beehive hairdos in the grand lobby.

What a fascinating place to people watch as we strolled through the hotel corridors and checked out the gaudy, over-the-top décor.

JULIANNA

Jess and Pete were up ahead while Ben and I fell back, holding hands. I'm glad Ben didn't say, "A penny for your thoughts" because I was thinking about what a girlfriend said to me the day before: "Are you guys ever going to get married?"

Quite frankly, I hadn't given the idea much thought. I mean, I was sure that we would get married, but I hadn't thought about *when* that would happen. I had enough sense to know that if we were to tie the knot, that would mean getting married during Ben's off-season, which was somewhere between the start of November to the end of January—just a three-month window. And since you need a good nine months to *plan* a wedding . . . .

I did the math. If Ben and I were going to marry during his next off-season, he needed to be asking me *now*. Otherwise, we would have to wait another year, and I wasn't about to wait another twelve months.

As we strolled hand in hand, I started getting impatient. I forgot how thoughtful Ben could be, how he weighs everything before taking action. *It's probably crossed his mind, Jules. Don't freak out.*

I dropped my hand out of Ben's warm clasp. I was kind of bummed just thinking about it. *We're never going to get married, are we? Instead, we'll just have this big long dating thing. We're never going to talk about it.*

Ben knew something was bothering me. "What's the matter?" he asked.

"You know what? Are you ever going to ask me to marry you? Because if you don't want to marry me, then let me know. Somebody asked me about it yesterday, and I didn't know what to tell her. Baseball season is coming up. So what are we doing?"

Ben took my hands into his. "Jules, look at me."

I dropped my eyes. I'm like, *Okay*—like when a parent asks you to look at them before he or she disciplines you. The last thing you want to do is look in that direction.

Ben was calm and resolute and asked me one simple question: "Jules, do you trust me?"

"Yes," and that was all that was said.

I felt ashamed of myself for allowing my emotions to get so far ahead of me. I wasn't being thoughtful of Ben and all of the care and leadership that he applied to our relationship. I was just being incredibly selfish, girly, and impatient.

I was really upset with myself for that.

BEN

When Julianna asked about marriage, I wanted to make her feel better by telling her something with more detail, but I knew I would have one shot to make the moment special, so I held my cards close to the chest.

Before I could propose, I knew I had to ask my future father-in-law, Jeff Gilmore, for permission to marry her. That was how it was done in our family and hers, I figured, so I understood that I needed to approach her father beforehand.

I saw an opening when Julianna traveled to California with a Belmont song-and-dance troupe called Company. Moments after I dropped her off at the Nashville airport, I phoned Jeff. I'll admit to some pre-call jitters, even though I knew Julianna's parents certainly approved of the match and loved having me around. Julianna's older sister and brother, Liz and Jeffrey Paul, already felt like *my* brother and sister.

After clearing my throat, I said, "Jeff, I would like to come see you and have a conversation about Julianna and our future together."

"That would be great," he said. "When would you like to get together?"

"Well, I was wondering if it could be this weekend. Julianna's in L.A. I'd prefer that she didn't know we're meeting."

"Sure, no problem."

I'm sure my future father-in-law knew *exactly* why I would drive eleven hours to Iowa City to see him.

Two days later, I hopped in my car, made the long drive from Nashville to Iowa City, and found myself sitting down with Jeff in the living room after the dinner dishes had been carried away.

"So, what brings you all this way?" I would imagine that Jeff, like any father whose beautiful daughter was being pursued by a suitor, enjoyed watching me squirm a bit.

I began by talking about Julianna and how I really enjoyed getting to know her during our relationship. Now I was ready to commit my life to her, I said. After proclaiming my love for her, I declared, "I'm here to ask you for her hand in marriage."

"I'm glad to hear that," Jeff said. "I thought you were going to ask for all of her, but you're just asking for her hand. Sure, you can have her hand."

I smiled—and felt every muscle relax. Jeff liked to kid people, so I answered in kind. "Well, I just want her hand right now for the ring, but later I would like the rest of her."

We shared a good laugh, but later in our conversation, he made it clear to me that he and Cheryl wanted Julianna to finish school and once we were married, that responsibility would fall on my shoulders as her husband. "There's one other thing," he added. "Julianna loves music, and we know she would love to pursue avenues that allow her to use her voice as well as her degree in music."

"I promise you that will happen," I said. "It's just as important to me as it is to you that Julianna uses her God-given gifts. I'll try to make it possible for her to do music, wherever we are."

That's why I didn't mind Julianna asking, in so many words, *Where's the ring?*

Little did she know that I had it all under control.

11

ROAD TRIP

JULIANNA

That semester, I had two classes in the afternoon, with the second one ending at 3:00 p.m. After I returned from the West Coast, we talked about taking Jess and Pete out to a fun place afterward, so Ben said he would make reservations at one of our favorite restaurants, the Melting Pot.

My two classes were back-to-back, which meant I had only ten minutes in between. I was always hustling to make my second class—a performance workshop—on time. The professor was a real stickler. She said if you miss two classes, then you'd get an automatic F. I had already missed one class period, so I couldn't miss another one.

I was walking into the school building when my cell phone chirped. Ben was trying to reach me.

"Hey, babe!" said a cheerful voice. "Come outside the building. I'm right here in my car."

I loved little surprises like this. I stepped outside, and there he was, parked in front of the school building, waiting for me. He rolled down his window. "How's it going?" he asked.

"Good. What are you doing here?"

"Come get in the car. I'm going to take you somewhere."

"Ben, I can't. My next class is in five minutes. I've already missed one, and if I miss again, I'll get an F."

"No, seriously, Jules, come get in the car. I want to take you somewhere."

"I really can't. I'd love to skip class, but that's not possible."

Then he turned serious. "Do you trust me?"

So, you're pulling the trust card again? "Yes, I trust you. We went over this yesterday at Opryland."

"Then get in the car."

Okaay . . . "Just so you know, I'm going to fail my performance class."

"Don't worry about it."

"So what are we doing?"

"You'll see. Look in the back. I brought some clothes for you."

My favorite jeans and a pair of tennis shoes were in the back seat, along with a purple country western blouse I had worn when we went line dancing a year ago. I hoped this wasn't an omen. I also wondered how he got some of my clothes.

We drove for thirty minutes. By this time, my class was half-way through. *I'm toast. I'm done. And where is Ben taking me anyway?*

I don't even know to this day what part of Nashville we were in when we pulled into a long gravel driveway leading to a large farm. Ben parked near a barn with horse stables inside. I love horses and considered myself a horse girl.

"What are we doing here?"

"We're going horseback riding," Ben explained.

He led me to the main house, where an older couple recognized Ben and welcomed us inside. I was told I could change in one of the bedrooms, which I did. When we were ready to go, the owners gave us two horses to ride. Ben's horse was a white stallion; I was handed the reins to a brown quarter horse.

I grew up riding horses, not a lot, but enough to feel comfortable around them. When I pulled myself up and into the saddle, I felt in control. Ben, on the other hand, struggled because his horse wasn't very obedient. I soon found out that these mounts weren't docile trail horses. These were working horses on a real farm.

Not only did Ben not know what he was doing, but his horse wasn't very well behaved. I teased him while we gently trotted down a dirt path toward the back 40, as they say. Ben did his best to smile, but he was busy concentrating on keeping his horse underneath him.

Suddenly, we heard gunshots go off. I looked up and saw neighbors unloading rounds at a makeshift target range. All the commotion spooked Ben's horse.

BEN

My horse freaked out and raised up on its hind legs. I hung on so that I wouldn't get bucked off, then did my best to calm down my horse. Once I felt it was safe to do so, I jumped off. I had enough horseback riding for the day. Plus, there was the risk of injury to consider.

I walked the horse back to the barn, holding his bridle the entire way. The horse fought me every step. To add insult to injury, I received gobs of horse slobber on my shirt.

JULIANNA

I was giving Ben all sorts of useful information: *Speak to him. Keep his head down. Tight grip.*

He had no idea how to handle a horse. But he was a good sport. When we got back in the car, we had a good laugh as we drove back to my apartment.

"I'll come back to pick you up at 5:30," Ben said. "We'll have a great time with Jess and Pete."

"See you soon."

I checked in with my roommates, Lindsay Wells and Kari Kragness, while I painted my nails at the kitchen countertop. When I stepped inside my bedroom with wet nails, there was a surprise waiting for me—a new dress lying on my bed. Attached was a note from Ben:

> *Jules,*
>
> *Wear this tonight.*
>
> *Love,*
>
> *Ben*

That was bold of him. He had purchased a V-necked black velvet dress that was beaded all the way to the floor. Very stylish.

I wanted to hold up the dress for a closer look, but then I remembered my nails were wet. I was pretty excited, though. This was shaping up to be a special night.

When 5:30 rolled around, Ben showed up in a dark suit, white shirt, and tie.

"You're looking handsome," I said. "Hey, I love my dress!"

"That's great to hear. Jess and Pete are driving their car, so we'll meet them at the Melting Pot."

Ben opened the passenger door, just like he always did. "We've got a little time before our reservation, so I thought we'd stop at Percy Warner Park on the way."

Percy Warner was one of my favorite parks in Nashville because of its equestrian center and picnic areas. A series of meandering roads led to the summit of a steep hill with a nice view of Music City. Ben had taken me there a week earlier, on Valentine's Day. We parked at the top and read our Bibles, talking about what we were reading and finishing in prayer.

We certainly weren't going to trek around Percy Warner Park since we were dressed in our finery. I guessed Ben was taking me there to admire the picturesque view and kill some time, but this side trip was out of character for him. He was the direct-route, do-not-pass-Go type of guy. When he gave off little clues—a forced laugh, a short response, and eyes darting around the road—I had a feeling that something was up.

When we arrived at the park, Ben turned and drove up the hill, which was one-way. A car was descending, which was weird . . .

"Hey, it's Matt and Phil. What are those guys doing here?" I said. Matt Toy was a good friend in town and Phil Carpenter was Ben's roommate.

"Ah, nothing. They're probably hanging out together." Ben slowed down to a crawl since the one-way lane was just a car-and-a-half wide. He didn't stop, though, but gave them a little wave as we passed.

Yeah, right. Matt and Phil show up at Percy Warner Park at the exact same time as we do, are driving the wrong way on a one-way road, and Ben is acting so weird. Something was totally happening.

BEN

When I saw Toy's car coming down the hill, my first thought was, *Oh, no. These guys are lost. They didn't follow my directions.* They were supposed to go into the park using a back road. Not only were they going the wrong way, but they were two guys that we both knew. *This could blow the whole thing right here.*

I had to play it cool. They stopped their car, but I kept right on going as I waved. Then I said to Julianna, "Those guys are so weird. What are they doing out here?"

JULIANNA

I knew something was up, but I didn't say anything to Ben. My intuition was confirmed when we arrived at the top and saw Jess and Pete's minivan. A big extension cord led from the vehicle to a small hill, where a white canopy had been erected.

BEN

I had purchased the white canopy that morning. I left my little brother Pete with the canopy, a Subway sandwich, and instructions to erect it on a small hill above the Percy Warner parking lot. He did a great job. Underneath the canopy was a table and two chairs. We needed electricity to power white Christmas lights.

I took Julianna's hand and escorted her to the table. She was bug-eyed, wondering what would happen next. Jessica handed us two menus and a Schedule of Events that included a recital of our dating history.

October 6/7: the first time we agreed to date
November 1: our first real date at the Reunion Tower in Dallas
December 28: our first kiss in the Gilmores' living room

JULIANNA

Ben was such the romantic. One month after our first date, on November 7, I received one rose from him. *Ah, that was really sweet. We've been dating one month. One rose.*

Ben had sent money to my friend, Lindsey Jones, asking her to buy a single rose and place it on my top bunk in my dorm room. The rose was accompanied by a note, which obviously had to be mailed a week before our "anniversary" date.

On December 7, I found two roses in the passenger seat of my car. On January 7, three roses in my dorm. Every month on the 7th, I could expect to find roses and a note from Ben somewhere I didn't expect it.

Ben finally stopped at one year and a dozen roses, but his thoughtfulness was indicative of how he would go the extra mile to make me feel special. And now, on top of Percy Warner Park, Ben had done it again.

Suddenly, Lindsey popped out from behind the canopy, carrying the same guitar she played in Dallas. She wore a beautiful dress trimmed with white lace.

She adopted a proper mien. "Ben and Julianna, welcome to your special evening. The wait staff will be bringing out the first course shortly. You have your menu and Schedule of Events in front of you. Now I would like to play a song I wrote for the two of you in honor of tonight."

She proceeded to play "My Love," which included these lyrics:

> *I'm giving you a love that's made forever*
> *A promise to remain right where you are*
> *And no one else is gonna love you better*
> *Cause you are my love, you are my love*

When Lindsey was done, she exited and two other girlfriends, Lindsay Wells and Kari Kragness, came around the corner with salads. The main course was a shrimp pasta prepared by Lindsey, a phenomenal cook. I learned later that she had made the meal earlier that day and brought it to Percy Warner. A warmer kept the meal hot.

Ben's younger brother Pete was part of the wait staff, keeping our water glasses filled. Ben and I really enjoyed the attention as well as the moment. As our dessert dishes were carried away, six more girlfriends announced their arrival and said they would be performing a series of skits.

One of them had a sign around her neck that said, "Benny Boo," which is what they called Ben. Another had a sign around her neck that said "Julesy."

They proceeded to act out several scenes, including the time we ran into each at the Daytona Beach hotel unexpectedly.

"I say that the reason Ben fell in love with me is because he saw my bikini fall off," announced "Julesy."

Ben—the real one—looked mortified. "No, that's not true!"

"Benny Boo" and "Julesy" then mimicked the both of us playing in the waves of Daytona Beach when suddenly a comber crashed on me, practically ripping my bikini top off. Of course, "Julesy" was dressed in regular clothes, so it was all done by pantomime.

"Benny Boo" turned his head like a gentleman, but then peeked to uproarious laughter.

My Ben protested. "I didn't see anything! I didn't even know she lost her top! She ducked under the water so fast."

This prompted another round of hilarity. Then Kari Kragness took the "Julesy" sign around her neck and reenacted our first kiss, which consisted of Kari tackling "Benny Boo" to the ground and pecking him on the lips.

We died of laughter. Before I knew it, though, the cast and crew gathered up the dishes and departed, leaving the two of us alone. I was flabbergasted by the extreme measures Ben had gone to make this a special evening.

In the quietness of the evening, he said, "I have one more thing for you." Then brought out the same old boom box.

I groaned. "You're not going to make me dance like you did at Dallas Baptist—"

"Just a couple of songs."

Ben led off with the same undanceable song he played on the baseball field at Dallas—as a joke. But that led quickly to several songs that we loved to listen to together.

What a wonderful moment, holding him close as we swooned to the slow music. And then the music stopped. Before I knew what was happening, Ben was on one knee. He pulled a ring box out of his pocket and opened it.

"Will you marry me?"

I didn't hesitate. "Yes, I will!"

He stood up, and we kissed and hugged each other close.

Then Ben said everyone was waiting for us at the bottom of the hill. We gathered up everything, drove down the hill, and accepted the well wishes from our friends.

BEN

On the way down, Julianna had a question for me: "What about the class I missed?"

"I thought you'd be wondering about that. I went to your professor and told her about my plans to propose to you. I mentioned that I knew you had already missed a class. Would she consider allowing you to miss another one? I think you know the answer to that question."

We started talking about a wedding date immediately. Our choices were few because of my baseball, but basically we talked about a December wedding. That would give Julianna and her family a good nine or ten months to plan the wedding. There was no doubt where we'd do the nuptials: her dad's church in Iowa City.

Then we zeroed in on December 17, 2005, because of the way the stars were aligned: it was a Saturday night, and December 17 was the date of my parents' wedding. Julianna and I asked Mom and Dad if that would be okay to "steal" their date, but of course they were thrilled.

A week after the proposal, I left Nashville for the Astros' spring training headquarters in Kissimmee, Florida. Even though I had led the New York Pennsylvania League in batting average, I was promoted one solitary rung to the low-Class A South Atlantic League, where I was assigned to the Lexington Legends in Lexington, Kentucky. Julianna drove up from Nashville to Lexington—it was around four hours one-way—to see me for the day on several occasions.

I played well for the Legends, batting .304, good enough to earn a mid-season promotion to the Astros' Class A-plus team, the Salem Avalanche in Salem, Virginia. One more step up the ladder.

The only time Julianna came to see me play in Salem was in August. She drove out with Lindsey Jones and stayed with some people I had gotten to know. I hadn't seen Jules in a month or so, so I really missed my fiancée.

There's a baseball tradition of ballplayers hitting on cute girls in the grandstands by lobbing them baseballs with messages written on them. Sometimes players write down their phone numbers and ask if they want to meet after the game. The messages, whether literal or implied, can be pretty blatant, if you catch my drift.

I had never participated in this tradition, of course, but with my fiancée at the game, I thought it would be fun to send a message to her. I got a baseball from one of the clubhouse guys and wrote the following on the ol' horsehide:

> *Hey, Hottie. I saw you sitting up there looking so fine, and I knew I just had to meet you. Got any plans after the game? I think I can show you a grand time. Oh, one more question. Do you want to get married?*
>
> *Signed, No. 6.*
>
> *P.S. 8:07 p.m.*

I was wearing number 6 at the time. Julianna was sitting five or ten rows behind the dugout. I stepped out, made eye contact with her, and softly tossed the ball underhand. She caught the ball with two hands, which was a minor miracle in itself.

JULIANNA

The message was so cute. I saw the *P.S. 8:07 p.m.* I looked at the scoreboard clock, which said the time was 8:02.

What does that mean, 8:07? I wasn't sure, but I had an inkling. I think Ben wanted me to meet him outside the clubhouse. We had joked about teammates who had clandestinely done that during a game. I got out of my seat and made my way through the concourse until I was standing outside the door leading to the clubhouse, hoping to see Ben.

BEN

Mind you, I was not playing this game. I had a sore knee that would eventually get operated on after the season. At any rate, no one was paying attention, so I left the bench for the clubhouse and snuck out the back door.

Julianna was waiting for me, and we totally made out for two minutes. If anyone had caught us, I would have been toast. The coaching staff would have reprimanded me for leaving the dugout during the game. Sure, it was a bit of a rebellious move, but we were in love and slightly crazy, so we were willing to take the chance.

I played 42 games for Salem and batted .333, which led the team, but on a balky knee that flared up during the season. It seems that I had partially torn the meniscus in my right knee, so I was ready to submit to arthroscopic surgery when the season was over. Then USA Baseball asked me to play on the 2005 World Cup team. Since the tournament started on September 2, during the final month of the major league baseball season, Team USA was made up of minor league prospects like myself. I was thrilled to be chosen. How many chances would I get in a lifetime to put on a USA jersey and play for my country?

The Baseball World Cup was held in the Netherlands, which turned out to be a great international experience. Even though Cuba won its ninth consecutive World Cup championship, I played well, put together a seven-game hitting streak, and had a team-best .500 on-base percentage.

My first trip to Europe . . . and playing for my country.

Very cool.

When I got home, I got my knee taken care of in preparation for the wedding. I also had to take care of a few other things—like paying for the honeymoon. Baseball fans read about the stratospheric salaries of major league players but aren't aware that minor league players can barely survive on their meager earnings. I still have the stub from my first paycheck from the Tri-City ValleyCats: I received $236.17 for two weeks of playing baseball. That's barely $500 a month, which was why I, along with the rest of my teammates, relied on Subway and Taco Bell as well as the tub of creamy peanut butter, jar of strawberry jam, and loaves of white bread that was set out for the players before and after each game. There were also bags of potato chips or nacho chips at this minor league version of "The Spread." And if we were lucky, there might be some fruit—apples or oranges.

Julianna and I talked about where we should honeymoon. We knew that a pricey resort in the Caribbean or Hawaii was out of the picture. I suggested San Diego, which wasn't known to be terribly warm in December, but Christmas time was off-season and flights were cheap from Chicago. As for a honeymoon retreat, we surfed the Internet and found an exotic listing for "Casa Bali" in Escondido, about twenty miles northeast of downtown San Diego. "Casa Bali" was the name of a small Indonesian house that had been shipped from Indonesia and built on a hill above the main house on the property.

Airline tickets and honeymoon resorts needed a credit card, but I didn't have one—even the generous credit card companies didn't consider me a good risk. I asked Dad if I could put everything on his card and pay him back, which was fine.

I was counting every dollar because I didn't have many to count. I needed a ring, so Julianna went ring shopping for me in Iowa City, where a jeweler had a titanium ring with a tangle of black-and-silver strands. Julianna thought it was the coolest ring ever.

"How much is it?" I asked from Eureka.

"They want $235," Julianna replied.

"No way! We're not spending $235 on my wedding ring!"

The next time we saw each other, we went ring shopping . . . on eBay. Julianna and I scrolled through web pages and found a titanium one that we liked. This price was more reasonable: $17.

When the titanium ring arrived a week before the wedding, it was huge—like two or three sizes too big. When I turned my hand over, the ring dropped to the floor. I knew this wasn't going to work, but I didn't have time to send the ring back and order a different one.

I returned to Illinois and showed my family the gigantic ring. I endured some good-natured teasing until my father took pity on my plight. "Let's go shopping tomorrow," he said.

Dad took me to Kay's Merchandise in Peoria. "Look, this is something that you're going to wear the rest of your life, so you have to get something nice. I'll take care of it."

I chose a nice-looking silver ring with engraved crosses around the band for $300. What Dad did endeared me to him once again. My parents didn't have a lot of money. They always lived paycheck to paycheck, raising five kids on a pastor's salary. Mom and Dad always made sacrifices for us and lived very frugally.

Their example was a reminder of what marriage was all about. Mom and Dad always told us kids that the Lord would always take care of us and we could depend on Him. Seeing them live that out gave me a great foundation to build on as I became one with Julianna.

I had no idea that the Lord had the highest highs and the lowest lows waiting for us.

INTENTIONAL WALK

JULIANNA

I always pictured a white, winter wedding in my childhood dreams, and a mid-December marriage in wintry Iowa is what we got.

What I didn't picture was buying *two* wedding dresses.

Let me explain. I was in Dallas visiting my sister Liz. She and Dan, along with their two boys, Luke and David, had moved to the Big D because Dan was hired as the assistant coach of . . . the Dallas Baptist baseball team. Talk about a small world.

Part of the fun of getting married is shopping for a dress. Liz and I stepped into a small bridal boutique in downtown Dallas, where we found a beautiful white dress in silk with a really deep V-neck front and plunging back. The $300 price tag was quite reasonable, so I bought the dress and had it altered to fit.

My wedding dress was shipped to Nashville, where I tried it on following the alterations. The more I looked in the mirror, the more I felt immodest. I think I was so excited about marrying Ben that back in Dallas, my emotions were spurred to find something sexy but tasteful. Unfortunately, I was clearly open to the world and clearly did not have my mother with me when I bought the revealing dress.

Since my wedding dress had been altered, I couldn't take it back, which was a major bummer, especially because I had spent my own money to purchase it. I had been working three part-time jobs throughout my college years at Belmont: I was a production manager for Women of Faith, a Christian women's organization that held weekend conferences around the country; I worked with a contemporary Christian music singer named Plumb, which was a stage name for Tiffany Lee; and I worked as a trainer at the campus fitness center.

I showed the dress to a seamstress in Nashville, but she shook her head. There was no way to alter the décolletage, which meant I wouldn't be presentable. I had written in a journal years earlier that I wanted my wedding dress to reflect my spiritual qualities as well as my physical attributes. I didn't feel my spiritual characteristics were on display when I wore this alluring wedding dress.

I started looking around for another wedding gown in Nashville and found a white strapless dress that I loved, but this one set me back another $600. I was kicking myself for making such a big mistake when Dad—like Ben's father with his wedding ring—stepped up to the plate and reimbursed me for the second wedding dress.

I woke up the morning of my wedding to a fresh blanket of snow covering the flat Iowa plains on a bright, sunshiny day. I still remember how the snow glistened and sparkled in the sun's rays.

Everything about the December day was perfect. I know I looked radiant as Dad walked me down the center aisle at Parkview Church on our wedding day. Waiting for us was Ben and his father,

Tom, who would marry us. There were plenty of witnesses—more than four hundred in attendance. Outside, a frosting of fresh snow made for a Currier & Ives tableau.

We had initially asked my dad if he wanted to officiate with my future father-in-law, but Dad said, "Walking you down the aisle will be enough."

BEN

Her father had a hard time handing Julianna away. You could see him battling his emotions. When my father said, "Who gives this woman to be wed to this man?", Jeff visibly paused for a long time—probably close to twenty seconds—before saying, "Her mother and I do." You could tell he was deeply moved about letting his daughter go.

We wanted songs, so Betsy Boyer, a college friend, and Tiffany Lee—Plumb—each sang a nuanced number. We had a Scripture reading. We lit a unity candle. We had our parents come up and pray with us. We heard a sermon from my dad, who loves to preach. He'd been preaching to me all his life, so in his mind, he was probably thinking *one last time.*

"You know, when you were a kid, I told you to stay away from girls because girls make your legs weak," Dad began with light laughter. "I said you wouldn't be as good of an athlete if you had a girlfriend. Well, that's not entirely true. If you find the right girl, she can make you stronger."

Dad always had great timing, and our wedding was representative of how we wanted the ideal marriage. We harbored the expectation that we would have the perfect relationship, the perfect wedding, and the perfect honeymoon.

Little did we know, in our naivety, that no marriage is perfect, but that revelation was yet to come.

As for our wedding night, that was pretty darn good. In case you're wondering, we were virgins when we checked into The Lodge Hotel in Bettendorf, Iowa, about an hour away from Iowa City.

When we speak to high school groups, we tell them that it *is* possible to wait, that not everyone is doing it, and that we speak from personal experience. It wasn't easy getting to the finish line with our purity intact, but we were able to give each other a priceless gift that could only be given once.

But Dad was right. Girls can make your legs weak.

JULIANNA

And guys can make you . . . okay, let's not go there, although I tell girls that wedding nights can be pretty uncomfortable when it's your first time. The thing that was undeniable was how the physical experience bonds you to somebody in a way that you can't bond with anyone else.

They say that some women who've been sexually abused in the past bring those issues to the marriage bed. Praise the Lord, that didn't happen on our wedding night. Anything that happened at age twelve wasn't in my head at all, which to me shows the Lord's healing and protection.

We slept in and took our time leaving for Chicago, where we had an early morning flight for San Diego the following morning. For our honeymoon, we wanted to go to some place warm. That meant that Florida certainly fit the bill, but I was born and raised in Orlando, so Florida had lost some of its luster. Neither of us had been to San Diego, so Southern California sounded like a fun alternative.

We had "Casa Bali" all to ourselves. The people who owned the home were also the chefs, so for breakfast, lunch, and dinner, they would bring our covered meal onto our patio, ring a bell, and slip into the shadows. We barely left the Casa, relaxing and doing what honeymooning couples do.

BEN

We moved into an apartment back in Nashville and settled into married life. I had promised Julianna's parents that she would graduate from Belmont, but we both decided that she should take off the spring semester so she could be with me during the baseball season. She would return to school in the fall to finish up.

I had been promoted to the Astros' Double A team in Corpus Christi, Texas. While I was at spring training in Florida, I inquired if there were any host families in Corpus Christi. Throughout the minor leagues, families will "adopt" a player for the summer, providing him with room and board and often a sense of belonging. Since I was married, that meant a host family would have to set the welcome mat out for the both of us.

Allen and Debbie Morris opened up their home and their hearts to us in Corpus Christi. They gave us an upstairs bedroom and run of the house. When I was gone on road trips, they made Julianna feel like part of the family.

This was Julianna's introduction to the minor league lifestyle, which was pretty bare bones since the players aren't paid much. She picked up a few much-needed dollars working part-time at the team store. When I was on the road, she worked on her music in our upstairs bedroom at the Morrises. My big wedding present to her was an M-Audio electric keyboard and stand, a microphone and mic stand, and a new iMac computer that she could use to compose songs. Sure, that was a major splurge that pretty much emptied my bank account, but I wanted to show Julianna that I cared about her future in music. I loved hearing the early work on a half-dozen songs or so, and Julianna told me she had plenty of other tunes in her head.

On the field, I got off to a fast start and was batting .327 midway though the season. When we rolled into Springfield, Missouri, to play the Cardinals affiliate, carloads of Zobrists made the drive to see me play since this was our closest series to my Illinois hometown. Since this was a mini Zobrist summer reunion, Julianna drove up from Corpus Christi.

We were staying in a Springfield hotel when the hotel phone jangled me awake at 8:00 a.m.—early for ballplayers.

The Astros assistant general manager was on the line, which woke me up in a hurry.

"Ben, we've decided to trade you and Mitch Talbot to the Tampa Bay Devil Rays for Aubrey Huff. I just want to thank you for your service to the organization and for the way you've played for us the last couple of years. We wish you all the best in your career. Someone from the Devil Rays will be calling you shortly."

I set the phone on the hook, stunned by the turn of events.

Julianna stirred awake. "What was that all about?" she asked.

"We've been traded. We're no longer part of the Houston Astros. We're with the Tampa Bay Devil Rays now."

"Who are the Devil Rays?"

That was a good question. I was oblivious to anything happening outside my world—the minor leagues. But I was shocked because I thought I was playing well for Corpus Christi. I hadn't learned yet that in the baseball world, sometimes you get traded because you're good, not because you're a bad player. The Devil Rays apparently *wanted* me because they accepted two minor league guys in exchange for Aubrey Huff, who was a fantastic major league hitter in the prime of his career.

Things happened in a hurry. The Devil Rays organization (the team would change its name to just the "Rays" with the start of the 2008 season) called and told me to get to Durham, North Carolina, as soon as I could. The Durham Bulls were the Devil Rays' Triple A affiliate. That was great news because the promotion meant I was one level away from the major leagues.

My family was disappointed to see me leave but ecstatic about the trade. There was more than me to think about—we had to get Julianna to Durham too. We put our heads together and came up with a complicated plan that involved Julianna and my father driving both of our cars from Corpus Christi to Durham. Fortunately, Dad had a vacation week from church.

JULIANNA

Tom followed in Ben's car while we drove straight through from Corpus Christi, stopping only at a roadside motel to grab some sleep. My father-in-law was so sweet; he got us two rooms so that I wouldn't feel uncomfortable. At 6:00 a.m. the next morning, I was knocking on his door, saying "Let's go!" I wanted to see Ben play his first Triple A game that night.

When we arrived at the ballpark, I saw a group of girls sitting in the same section as me. They looked like players' WAGs—wives and girlfriends. *Do I introduce myself?* I was kind of nervous.

I worked up my courage and approached a group of five, and they couldn't have been more welcoming. Then I returned to my seat next to Tom. We were hungry and decided to get something to eat. When we stood in line to pick up our hot dogs, we both noticed a sign for "Mike's Hard Lemonade."

We agreed that slushy lemonades sounded refreshing on a warm summer's night. When we asked for a pair of hard lemonades, the vendor sized up the two of us. "You know, there's alcohol in these lemonades."

My father-in-law and I shared a good laugh and ordered Cokes instead.

BEN

Most newlywed wives would be complaining about having to move again, saying *Will I make any friends?* or *Where are we going to live?* Julianna wasn't like that at all. She embraced the move and even went with the flow when our bank account dipped to $32.08. It turned out that my last paycheck from the Houston Astros was taking forever to reach us in Durham, and getting on the Bulls' payroll involved dealing with bureaucracy. We had gone four weeks without a paycheck.

JULIANNA

We were really low on money. We had moved into a three-bedroom apartment with two other players and their significant others, and I can remember sitting at the kitchen table with those girls, calling banks and trying to get a credit card. No one would give us a credit card because we had no credit. We were using a bank debit card to pay for everything, but when there's only $32 left in your account . . .

We had gotten used to being poor and scraping by. Date Night on Ben's day off was something important to us, so we improvised. One time in Corpus Christi, we stopped by the Dollar General store and bought a kite for $1 and flew the kite along the wind-swept beach. On another occasion, we bought a tent for $5 and camped out.

One time in Corpus Christi, a fan came up to Ben after a game and handed him an envelope. "There's a little gift card for you," the fan said.

Ben opened the envelope, which contained a $25 gift card for Chili's. When Ben showed me, I screamed, "Yeah! We get to go on a real date!"

Early that afternoon, after failing to get approved for a credit card, I drove Ben to the Durham Bulls stadium in his car. Typically, Ben would take his car to the field and I would come later in my vehicle, but we couldn't do so because my fuel tank was on empty. We just couldn't afford to put any gas into my car.

Ben pulled into the gravel lot across the street from the stadium. We discussed our serious situation and how we were really out of money. Talk about depressing. I started crying. The pressure of trying to keep us afloat had gotten to me.

Ben reached over and drew me close. We hugged each other for the longest time. Then he closed his eyes and prayed out loud:

"Lord, You know exactly where we are at this moment. You know that we have been faithful to You. We trust You with our finances and ask that You provide just as You have always done. We pray this in Your name, amen."

Ben pulled away to leave. "I'm going to run into the clubhouse and see if I got paid. Stay here and I'll be right back."

I waited in the car for a couple of minutes. Sure enough, he ran back out, waving a white envelope in his hand. "We got paid!" he was yelling.

"Yeah," I cheered. We were so excited because once again, God had provided for us. The check was for $1,000, which made us feel like millionaires.

"You better get this to the bank," Ben said.

We kissed each other goodbye, and I left the parking lot totally pumped because I was driving to Bank of America to immediately deposit what felt like a windfall.

BEN

I returned to the clubhouse to prepare myself for the game that night. I would have been excited to go to any Triple A team, but the Durham Bulls were one of the best known minor league teams in the country because of two films: *Bull Durham*, a 1988 movie starring Kevin Costner and Susan Sarandon, and the more recent *The Rookie*, a 2002 film starring Dennis Quaid as Jim Morris, a true story about a thirty-five-year-old pitcher who was called up from the Bulls to pitch in the major leagues for the very first time.

Just like in the movies, there was a Durham Bull sign beyond the outfield fence. If you hit the smoke-snorting bull with a home run, you won a steak dinner at a local restaurant. Until the paycheck arrived, I was thinking of swinging for the fences that night. A steak dinner with all the trimmings would sure beat a cold peanut-butter-and-jelly sandwich in the clubhouse.

That night, July 31, 2006, would be my nineteenth game with the Bulls since arriving from Corpus Christi. I was batting .304 and had gotten on base 22 times in 11 games, so I was playing good ball.

I was stretching in the outfield when our manager, John Tamargo, approached me. "Ben, you gotta go," he said.

"Go where?"

"You gotta go because you're going to the big leagues!"

"Are you serious?"

"The trading deadline ended today, and the big club shipped Julio Lugo to the Dodgers. There's an opening at shortstop, so you're being called up. Pack your bags. Your flight leaves in two hours."

I felt lightheaded. What a moment! Especially on a day like this, when we had woken up with $32 to our names. We had prayed for the Lord's provision, and within a matter of minutes, we received a $1,000 check and then a promotion to major league baseball, where I'd not only get a chance to play baseball at the highest level but receive a huge bump in salary—to something like $2,000 *a day*.

JULIANNA

After dropping by Bank of America, feeling great about being solvent again, I was on my way back to the apartment when Ben called.

"Jules . . ."

The long pause wasn't like Ben. "What? What's the matter?"

"We're going to the big leagues."

"You've got to be kidding!"

"No, I'm not. I'm leaving for the airport right now."

After catching my breath, we talked about how I should get to Tampa. We were too new to major league baseball to know that Ben could have called the Rays traveling secretary and arranged for our cars to be shipped to Tampa. Instead, we decided that I had to drive so that we'd have a car in Tampa. That meant getting on the road right away. No way I was going to miss Ben's major league debut.

As soon as I got off with Ben, I raced back to our little apartment, shoved our stuff in my car, and headed south on 1-95. I called Dad and must have talked to him for hours en route. Fueled by two Cokes and lots of anticipation, the nearly 700-mile journey would take eleven hours, but I arrived safely at 4:00 a.m. at Ben's hotel.

BEN

Talk about a whirlwind. I raced to the Durham airport, where Southwest Airlines had an early evening nonstop to Tampa. Upon landing, I checked into a hotel for the night.

The next afternoon, I headed over to Tropicana Field. The first thing I noticed was the lineup card on a tack board as I turned a corner to enter the clubhouse. I scanned the names until my eyes rested on "Zobrist SS" penciled in the No. 9 slot. My heart skipped a beat, but I was excited.

"Joe wants to see you," said one of the bench coaches who introduced himself.

That would be Joe Maddon, whose black, thick-rimmed glasses spawned a "Joe Maddon Retro Glasses Giveaway" earlier that season. The Rays manager was trying to turn around an expansion team that never won more than seventy games into a winner that could compete in the AL East, the major's best division populated by the New York Yankees and Boston Red Sox.

"Welcome to the big leagues," Joe said with a wink. "You ready to go?"

"Of course."

"Foley will get with you on the signs. Other than that, I just want you to go out there and enjoy yourself. Just do the same things you've been doing in the minor leagues, and you'll be fine."

"Thanks, Joe." In professional baseball, one of the first things they teach you is that you don't call the manager "Skipper" or coaches "Coach." You call them by their first name or nickname. There is no "Sir" or "Mister" in pro ball either.

I didn't say much, but I could hardly contain the adrenaline inside. I don't know who was more excited that I had made it to the big leagues—myself, Julianna, or my family, who had flown in that day from Illinois, along with a few of my best friends. Dad, Mom, and my two younger brothers, Pete and Noah, would be sitting with Julianna on this special day. August 1 also happened to be the twelfth birthday of Noah, so there was a lot to celebrate.

Talk about a promise kept. Mom and Dad had always said that they would be there for my first major league game. Mom was my biggest fan in the stands before Julianna.

She and Dad, along with my brothers and Julianna, witnessed my major league debut against the Detroit Tigers, but I went hitless that night. My family stayed all week, but it wasn't until my fourth game when I snapped an 0-for-14 streak with my first major-league hit, a single to right-center off Boston pitching ace Curt Schilling. The ball was tossed to our clubhouse manager for safekeeping and given to me later.

I smacked my first major-league home run two nights later against Red Sox pitcher Jason Johnson in the second inning. Later in the game, we were down 6–2 when my two-run double in the seventh inning ignited a rally that would end with a 7–6 victory.

I loved being part of "The Show," as ballplayers referred to the major leagues. Everything was first class all the way: travel, hotels, ballparks, clubhouse food, and per diem money. The major league minimum salary of $327,500, which was prorated, of course, was fifteen times more than I made in Durham.

I played in fifty-two games, batting .224 and hitting two home runs. A good start, but I thought I could play better once I got more experience. One highlight was participating in a rare 2–6–2 triple play when Raúl Ibáñez of the Seattle Mariners came up with runners on first and third and nobody out. When Ibáñez struck out on a swing-and-a-miss, the first base runner, Adrian Beltre, was trying to steal second on the pitch. I covered second and took the catcher's throw. When Beltre saw he was going to be out by ten feet, he stopped and tried to run back to first base. I ran him down and made the tag as Mariners' runner José Lopez broke for home. I pivoted and fired a strike back to the plate, where the tag was made for the third out.

The 2006 season was a whirlwind. I started at the Double A level with Corpus Christi, unsure what my status was as a prospect. Then I was traded to the Devil Rays organization, called up a few weeks after playing on their Triple A affiliate, and overnight became part of the conversation regarding Tampa Bay's future. Even though we had another hundred-loss season, finishing 61–101 and last in the AL East standings, the future looked bright. It looked like I had a home at shortstop.

I knew how fortunate Julianna and I were to be in this position. We had friends and knew people in the minor leagues who had struggled for years to break the glass ceiling. To a certain degree, we both felt, *God, why did You bless us this way?*

Little did we know that we were about to go through a series of trials that would test our faith in God—and in each other.

PIVOT PLAY

BEN

Tampa Bay asked me to play Fall Ball in Arizona for more seasoning, which I agreed to do. Julianna returned to Belmont and flew out every Thursday night to spend a three-day weekend with me in Phoenix.

We finally had some money in the bank, which we used to pay off Julianna's outstanding college loans as well as tuition for her final semester in the fall of 2006. Getting rid of debt really felt good as did Julianna graduating from Belmont in December. Instead of walking with her class, we celebrated her degree in commercial voice *and* our first wedding anniversary by taking a second honeymoon. Just before Christmas, we flew to Paradise Island in the Bahamas for several days at the Atlantis resort, where we had a great time on the water slides and took plenty of excursions.

You could say that life was perfect.

My manager Joe Maddon told the media that he was going with me at shortstop, so I was feeling secure about my spot on the team, so secure that at the start of spring training, I decided to get a truck and move the furniture inside our Nashville apartment to Tampa Bay so that we'd have our stuff for the next seven months.

Three weeks into the 2007 season, however, I was really struggling at the plate. I'm usually a slow starter, but staying underneath the so-called "Mendoza line"—players who can't hit above a .200 batting average—meant that I wasn't helping the team. A .160 batting average, or a "buck-sixty" as they like to say on *ESPN SportsCenter*, made me a liability on the field.

I tried to make up for my shortcomings at the plate by making plays in the infield, but I pressed and committed several uncharacteristic fielding errors that cost our team. I was sat down, replaced by one of our utility players, Brendan Harris, who made enough timely hits to keep me on the bench.

A couple more weeks went by, and I was still riding the pine. Joe called me into his office while we were playing a road game in Baltimore. He didn't beat around the bush. "Ben, we want you to play, but Brendan's been hitting the ball, so we're sending you down. You work on your game in Durham, keep developing as a player, and you'll be back up in no time," said my manager.

Even though I should have been expecting the demotion, the news hit me like Tropicana Field's domed roof falling on my head. Emotionally, I was squashed.

This was the first time in my life that I'd ever been demoted. Ever since my father underhanded Wiffle ball pitches in our living room, the trajectory of my life had always been on the rise. There had never been any speed bumps. No declines in my athletic ability, no *You didn't make the team* or *You're not starting*. I was always starting. I was always going up. I was always one of the best players on the field.

The demotion was a huge blow, not only to my pride and confidence, but to my faith as well. Just when I was starting to feel settled in the major leagues, God switched things up in a big way. This wasn't in the plan—at least my plan. Couldn't God see that?

My family had made plans to come see me play in Tampa Bay. Plane tickets had been purchased, hotel rooms reserved. What was going to happen now? What were we going to do with all the furniture and boxes we had brought down to Tampa? Now I had to drag my wife back to Durham and live on a minor-league salary, which meant sharing a dingy apartment with one or two other baseball couples. Bus trips instead of plane rides. Subway sandwiches instead of Ruth's Chris marbled steaks. Schlepping my bags to the Days Inn instead of opening the heavy door to my five-star room at the Westin and seeing my bags already on the luggage rack.

Fear and anxiety crept in, causing a chain-reaction of negative thoughts. Maybe I wasn't cut out to be a major league baseball player. Maybe my game didn't measure up. Maybe I was one of those players who would bounce back and forth from the minors to the majors and vice versa, never good enough to stick with the parent club. Was this something I really wanted to do?

One night, after being sent down to Durham, I was standing at my shortstop position, smoothing the infield with my cleats between pitches. Suddenly, a surge of anxiety surged over me like a breaking wave at Daytona Beach. I began breathing heavily. Rivulets of sweat rolled down my forehead and into my eyes. I had to gulp air into my lungs.

I pulled myself together for the next pitch, only to have these feelings of anxiety swarm all over me again. When they got so bad that I felt like I would pass out, I squatted between pitches to gather myself. I hoped that my teammates or coaches on the bench didn't notice how I was fighting my body out there at deep short.

The anxious moments eventually passed, but they always returned and clamped on to me like ankle weights. Each time I thought I was over the hump, the anxiety attacks struck with a vengeance. The lows became lower. The depths became deeper.

What I would find out later was that, medically speaking, I was experiencing classic anxiety attacks. They are not uncommon; anxiety/panic disorders affect around 40 million American adults every year, or close to one-in-five persons. Sure, anxiety is a normal human emotion that everyone experiences from time to time, but this was different. These anxiety attacks were causing such distress that they were interfering with my ability to play baseball—or lead a normal life. No matter how hard I tried to overcome my worries or fears, they just wouldn't go away.

One time I was talking to a Christian friend about signing autographs and handing out testimony cards before games. During autograph sessions, I liked to leave each kid or adult with a baseball-like card that had our bio and stats on the front and the gospel message on the back.

I told my friend I couldn't handle the strain any longer. "I don't feel like signing today," I said.

He knew that was uncharacteristic of me because I usually signed before every game and handed out testimony cards regularly. When I further explained that I didn't have it in me, he stopped me. "You're in a spiritual battle," my friend pointed out.

"Nah. I'm just struggling today."

"Satan's trying to keep you from doing God's will for your life. You can't let him get the best of you. Maybe there's someone in Durham that God wants you to impact tonight."

He had a point, but I didn't need additional spiritual pressure piled on my sagging shoulders. I needed rest in God. I needed peace in my own situation, but I didn't have it.

To maintain my equilibrium, I put on a familiar façade in front of family and friends. *We're going to be back up there soon. God is going to take care of us.* I was saying all the right things, but deep down, I felt nothing but anxiousness and worry. I feared for the future and didn't trust in the Lord. Even after all God had done for me and clearly had provided for me in the past, I couldn't find it within myself to actually trust in Him at that moment. I was lost, and the only person who knew what was going on was Julianna. Yet I held back my innermost thoughts of doubt from her.

JULIANNA

We'd been married nearly eighteen months, so I was getting pretty good at reading Ben's moods. Up until we got sent down, he didn't really have any bad moods and was always chipper. But when Ben got demoted to Triple A, these anxiety episodes started cropping up. He wasn't upbeat at all. He seemed down when it was just the two of us.

I didn't notice the panic attacks in the field, but I observed significant changes in his sleeping and eating habits. Regarding the former, he tossed and turned at night, restless and half awake. On some days, he laid around in bed until it was time to go to the ballpark. When I accompanied him on a road trip, the first thing Ben did when we entered our hotel room was to draw the curtains and make the room as dark as possible.

"Why do you want to do that?" I asked.

"The light hurts my eyes," he replied.

As for food, he barely ate above a subsistence level. I never knew if he was going to take more than a bite of his sandwich or a forkful of pasta. Then I really became concerned when Ben said that he couldn't taste his food.

BEN

We'd go out to eat at an Italian restaurant, and Julianna would say, "Oh, this pizza is so good," but I'd pick at my food and push my plate away.

"I can't taste any flavors," I said. I had lost my appetite.

Barely eating and being fatigued 24/7 turned me into a miserable person. I would sleep in and wake up with no energy. The reason I was drained was because I didn't see anything good coming out of this situation.

Everything I saw through my day was through dark-colored glasses. I was thinking so negatively and so pessimistically about everything that I was blind to the blessings around me. I even tried to copy down all the blessings in my life in a journal, but that didn't work. I also tried hard to think positively, which would help for a couple of days, but then I got tired and the negative thoughts would inevitably return.

I didn't like myself and knew I was being extremely selfish, but I didn't care. It was all about me and my problems, and that's all I talked about with Julianna. What I was doing was taking some of the extra weight on my shoulders and placing those burdens directly on hers.

Teammates didn't want to go out to dinner with us because I was a big grump. I was even a jerk to my family. One time they came to see me play on the road, but when we had a meal together, I sat there like a bump on a log, silent and uncommunicative. I was doing everything I could to be normal, but the reality is that I had all these things swirling around in my mind. I even questioned basic things about God:

God, do You really care for me?

God, do You really want what's best for me and Julianna in this situation, or am I making this all up?

Do I really have control of my life, or do You have control? Because if I have control, I'm a little bit worried right now.

Bottom line, I was putting a ton of pressure on myself and trying to be this perfect person I thought I was—and *should* be. I had never used a swear word growing up—even though you hear tons of cussing in baseball and it's almost expected in the clubhouse—because I wanted to be *perfect*. Maybe I had thought about using a few choice words in the past, but I had never uttered them in some kind of quixotic quest for perfection.

But as I sadly realized, no one is perfect, and that included me. As I looked around trying to make sense of my life, everything seemed to be crumbling beneath my feet.

JULIANNA

In the midst of this trauma, I accompanied Ben on a road trip to Indianapolis. Actually, I flew in and waited for Ben to arrive at the team hotel.

BEN

We travel by bus in Triple A, for the most part. I think we were coming in from Louisville or Columbus, and I was talking to a couple of teammates about how much trouble I was having sleeping.

"Dude, have a beer or a couple of glasses of wine before you go to bed," one teammate said. "That'll help you sleep."

My teammate was a Christian, so I wondered if he had figured out the truth: I was a I'm-Going-to-Be-Perfect, Never-Have-a-Drink kind of guy. I was twenty-five years old, and I couldn't remember intentionally swigging a beer, tasting a glass of wine, or sipping a mixed drink in my life.

"Tell you what," my teammate said. He unzipped his backpack. "Here, take this," handing me a Coors Light.

Even though I felt like I was accepting contraband, I stashed the beer can into my carry-on bag.

When Julianna and I were reunited at the hotel that night, I showed her the Coors Light. I don't think I ever saw her eyes get that big, but she quickly regained her cool.

"So, should I or should I not drink this beer?" I asked. This wasn't a rhetorical question. Julianna knew, given my state, that I was being completely honest with her, which I think she appreciated.

"Well, it's fine with me," she said. We had talked about her drinking wine in the past with her family, but out of respect for me, she hadn't sipped any alcohol since we exchanged our wedding vows. "If you want to have a drink, then have a drink," she said.

I popped the lid.

"Wait! I want a photo of this." Julianna searched her purse for her iPhone.

She snapped a shot while I slowly sipped my beer. We made light of the situation, but if I was expecting some huge major change in my life or spiritual revelation, that didn't happen. I didn't suddenly sleep like a baby or anything, but I slept longer for the first time in weeks and had a late but light breakfast with Julianna. We were looking for something to do when I suggested going to see a movie. Taking in a matinee was one of our favorite pastimes on the road.

JULIANNA

On this particular afternoon, a romantic comedy looked promising. "Let's go see that," I said. "It'll be fun to get your mind off baseball." *Let's laugh.*

"I suppose you're right," Ben said.

We sat down in the movie theater, sharing a tub of popcorn. We weren't twenty minutes into the movie when Ben stood up. "I can't watch this movie," he said. "I gotta go."

Is this really happening? I'll never forget following him into the lobby and asking, "What's going on?"

"I can't focus my attention on a movie right now."

We stepped outside and kept walking. Where we were going, I had no idea, but we spotted a plaza with some sort of natural history museum. Ben led us toward a plot of grass next to the museum, where he plopped down and started picking at the blades.

"How are you doing?"

Instead of answering me, Ben clenched his fist and looked to the heavens. "I can't take this!" he screamed at sky. "Why is this happening to me?!"

Ben was really upset, but witnessing him go off was disconcerting. He yelled more stuff at God, like how he had always done everything He'd asked him to, so why was he going through this personal hell? Then he fell back in the grass and beat the ground with his fists, wailing about his plight.

I couldn't take it any longer. As a wife, I had been trying hard to be supportive for weeks, but now we had entered the Nebuchadnezzar zone, with Ben figuratively chewing on the grass. "I'll see you back at the hotel," I muttered.

Ben showed up thirty minutes later. No angry words were exchanged, but our intense yet frustrating conversation can be summed thusly:

What's going on?

I don't know!

BEN

I had to get to the ballpark. That night, I played my most unfocused game yet. Even though I felt like a zombie out there, I wasn't playing that bad, however. I still got my share of hits.

Afterward, we went back to the hotel, which had a TGI Friday's downstairs. Julianna was famished, but I wasn't hungry because I was still in my pick-at-my-food stage. The lack of nutrients was taking a toll: when I had weighed myself in the Indianapolis clubhouse before the game, I was down to 198 pounds, a loss of twelve pounds of muscle. That was the lightest I'd been in years, and I know it was because of my depressed eating habits.

Great, I thought. *Am I going to waste away?* I wasn't sure if I was going to order anything, but I understood that Julianna needed some food in her stomach.

We scanned the menus. "Do you care if I have a margarita?" she asked.

I looked over the top of my laminated menu. She had never made that type of request before. "Look, I had a beer last night, so I don't care. Go ahead and have a margarita."

She ordered a blue margarita, and when the festive drink arrived in the typical birdbath-sized glass, she offered me a sip.

Whatever. I tried her margarita. Maybe I had three or four sips. But that was it.

That night, as I fell asleep, I realized that *not* drinking had become some sort of idol to me. It was something I was proud of, made me better than the next person, but I had to let go of that pride and the pressure to be perfect.

The following day, my family arrived in Indianapolis to see me play. They were excited to see me take the field and cheer me on. I helped my cause by hitting a home run, which they were pumped up and excited about. I should have been happy, but I wasn't smiling. I was still miserable.

I remember talking to my dad after the Indianapolis series, standing next to the team bus, and saying, "I'm not having fun at all. This is not what I dreamed of." He knew I was talking about the demotion from the big leagues.

"Ben, you've been struggling with baseball, and that's okay. You'll get through this. It's a season of your life, just a short time. You'll come out of it." He was trying to encourage me.

I hoped that I would turn things around, but I didn't know if that was possible based on my mental state.

Several weeks later, I was still sleeping three hours a night, waking up with eyes wide open and staring at the ceiling for hours. Insomnia, coupled with my anxiety attacks, coupled with losing weight and not wanting to eat, were physical manifestations of the mental issues I was going through at the time. I was trying to find myself, identify who I really was. The funny thing is that I was hitting the ball okay, batting around .280, and making plays from the shortstop position, yet I was still wallowing in misery.

I couldn't take much more of this. I called one of my best friends, Josh Costello. We've been tight ever since we were teammates on the Mexico missions trip. He'd supported me and I'd supported him in the past. He read Scripture at our wedding and knew us from the beginning of our relationship.

He offered to drive over from his place in Nashville and spend time with me in Louisville when we were playing the Cincinnati Reds affiliate. About forty-five minutes before game time, after batting practice, Josh phoned me to let me know that he had arrived in the stadium parking lot.

I told him to meet me at a certain door leading to the clubhouse. When Josh arrived, he stepped inside the long hallway leading to the clubhouse. No one was in sight.

"Thanks for coming, man," I said. "I see you found the door okay." We shared a quick hug.

"Good to see you," Josh replied. "I've been worried about you."

That was all the nudge I needed to release a torrent of tears. I really let it go and cried hard. All the frustration of dealing with my anxiety came out emotionally. My close friend reminded me that everything was going to be okay.

Quite frankly, if any of my teammates or coaches had stepped out of the clubhouse and looked down the long hallway, they would have thought I'd just learned some horrible news, like an unexpected death in the family. Instead, I was grieving for what my life had become. At that moment, I had a bona fide emotional meltdown.

Josh gave me another hug. "All you can do is hang in there and trust in the Lord," he said.

Josh was patient and encouraged me throughout that weekend. He listened to my ramblings, and when exhaustion had set in late that night, he slept on the floor of my hotel room and was a sounding board when we got up in the morning.

I remember the last game of the Louisville series on July 30, 2007. Right before the first pitch, I got pulled out of the lineup. My manager, Charlie Montoyo, told me that I was being called back up to the big leagues. "Congratulations," he said. "I hope you stay up there."

I was batting .279, so I wasn't tearing up the league, but the Devil Rays needed help in the infield.

I mumbled thanks to my manager, but there was no broad smile on my lips. My reaction was nothing like the one a year earlier, when I was thrilled to be called up. This time around, I wondered if I had what it takes to play at the major league level. *Are you setting yourself up for another fall?*

After the game, I met Josh back at the hotel and told him the news. "Ben, this is great. Be encouraged. God is going to bless you through this. Don't worry about a thing," he said.

The next morning at 6:00 a.m., Josh drove me to the Cincinnati airport for my flight to Tampa. I had called Jules from the ballpark right after I got the news, so she was flying from Durham and would meet me in Tampa.

We checked into the team hotel, which is the Vinoy Renaissance, a shiny Marriot property on Tampa Bay in St. Petersburg. The club paid for the first seven nights, and then you had to find your own accommodations.

So consider the situation. We were staying in a luxurious five-star hotel with 600 thread-count linens made from Egyptian cotton, receiving a generous per diem to buy expensive meals, and pocketing a huge salary bump to $56,000 a month. Yet my thoughts were these:

I don't want to go to the ballpark. I don't care about baseball. Why am I playing this game? I wish I could go home.

I voiced those thoughts to Julianna and added that I didn't want to have any responsibilities at this time.

JULIANNA

What Ben was going on and on about was really starting to get to me. At this point, I still hadn't told anybody anything, which meant we were both carrying this burden completely alone, with the exception of Joshua Costello. Even though I didn't know how much Cos knew, I didn't care at this point.

The way I looked at things, if I was with Ben, I wasn't helping. If I wasn't with Ben, I wasn't helping. It really didn't matter where I was because I couldn't help him get through this anxiety thing.

That night, after 11 o'clock, I slipped out of bed, tiptoed into the marbled-floored bathroom, and shut the door. In my hands were hotel stationery and a pen.

I thought about leaving Ben and going to be with my family. I could hang out with them until this all blew over. All I wanted was to be back in the corn.

I started a letter:

> *Dear Ben:*
>
> *I'm not leaving you. I'm too Christian to do that, but I can't be here any longer. I'm going to take a break and go home for a while. What's happening between us is affecting my spirits, affecting my soul, and affecting who I am. I can't be around all this negativity. You're going to have to figure this out on your own.*

I wondered what to write next. When I reread my words, I realized how scary it was that I actually felt this way. *Don't go there, Jules.* I ripped up the letter quickly and tossed the square bits into the Vinoy toilet. Then I flushed everything down the drain.

We needed help, and I knew enough as a pastor's kid that when you're in trouble, you call your pastor.

Our pastor was Bryon Yawn of Community Bible Church in the south part of Nashville. Byron had done our premarital counseling, so I thought he knew us pretty well. Even though it was well past 11:00 p.m., this was an emergency. Our marriage was on the rocks, so I went to my Contacts list and phoned him.

I didn't know if Bryon was asleep or even had his cell on, but to his credit, he took my call. The moment he said, "Hey, Julianna," I started bawling.

"Are you okay? What's going on?"

"I'm not okay. And Ben is not okay."

I'll never forget what Byron said to me. "For better or for worse, huh? Is this the worst part?"

"Yes, this is the worst part."

"Do you know now that Ben is just a man?"

"Yes, I now realize that Ben is just a man."

That was really it. That's all it was.

I explained to him briefly what was happening: Ben couldn't sleep. He couldn't taste food. He was fighting anxiety attacks on the field.

"We need to get Ben on the phone," he said.

Ben was in the bedroom—the completely pitch-black bedroom since Ben liked it that way. He was lying on the bed, looking at the ceiling when I opened the bathroom door.

"Byron wants to talk to you," I said.

BEN

I had heard Julianna talking in the bathroom and pretty much knew what the conversation was about with our pastor.

So, things were coming to a head. In some ways, I was glad that we could stop pretending that everything was fine. I accepted the phone, and Byron, a godly man who had done a great job with our premarital counseling, got straight to the point.

"What's happening, Ben?"

"Byron, I don't even want to go to work tomorrow. I don't want to go to the field."

He drew a long breath. "Ben, go to the field. Do your job. Then come back to the hotel to Julianna again. I'll be there tomorrow night to see you."

"I'm leaving tomorrow afternoon for Boston."

"Then I'll come to Boston," my pastor said. "But if you need me in Tampa tomorrow morning, I'll take the first flight out."

"No, that will be okay," I said, and then I shared with him the name of the team hotel. "You can stay with me since Julianna's not making the trip. I'll make sure there are two beds in the room," I said.

JULIANNA

I didn't want to go to Boston anyway.

BEN

When I arrived in Boston at dinner time, Byron was already waiting for me at the team hotel. We walked to a neighborhood restaurant and began the dialogue.

I shared all the weird things going on in my head. "Am I going crazy?" I asked. "What's happening to me?"

"What you're going through at this moment is totally normal," he assured me. "There are many people who find themselves getting depressed. You're not the first person to experience something like this."

Byron helped me to see that I was a mere mortal who looked at himself as a superhero. "And Julianna thinks you're a superhero too," he added. "But the reality is that you're just a man with issues and problems, just like any one of us walking the streets tonight. You're not perfect, nor will you ever be. You can't hold up this image of yourself any longer. Real life means real struggles, and that's what you're going through at this time."

Byron then shared some personal stories about tragedies that he'd been through to show me what I was going through. Going up and down to the major leagues was part of the natural cycle of life, he said, no different than any other mortal who'd trodden this Earth.

For the next two days, we talked at length before and after our games at Fenway Park. Byron counseled me to stop sharing every qualm or worry that crossed my mind with Julianna. Sure, I might fail at some things, but I needed to stop beating a dead horse by continuing to dwell on them in conversation with Jules.

But it was something that Byron said just before he left for the airport that really stuck with me:

"You need to repent."

"Me?" I replied.

"You need to repent of your selfish, self-consuming attitude right now, which is that you're more concerned about yourself than you are about your wife," he said. "You're more concerned about holding up this image about who you're supposed to be rather than loving Christ and adoring Him as your Savior. In other words, it's all been about you. But if you sacrifice your own life, your own self, for the betterment of Julianna and others, you'll come out of this the way you want."

Byron gave me something to chew on. I wasn't there yet, but my focus on perfection and having a perfect image was like a dog chasing its tail: I could try as hard as possible, but I'd never get there. There were more important things than playing baseball, and that started with my relationship with God and with Julianna.

Instead of seeing the demotion for what it was—hopefully something temporary and something to learn from—I allowed my confidence to be shattered. This was the first time I set my heart and my mind to do something and couldn't do it. But the issue was bigger than that. The Lord was trying to show me that I had allowed success to become an idol in my life. I wanted success on the baseball field more than I wanted Him.

I had to learn that God was using this teachable moment to show me that my heart was not really for Him or what He wanted. I remember saying this to the Lord:

Lord, what do You want? Whatever it is, I want to be faithful with that. I am committed to You and to using whatever talents You've given me so that I can glorify You. If You want me to play in Triple A, I'll do it with joy. If You want baseball to end and for me to go back to Nashville and get a normal job, then I'll do that, too.

I just want to be faithful, God, because I know I'm not guaranteed anything. If I could just stop trying to plan how things should go and just submit my heart, my life, my gift, my talent, my abilities, and even my relationship to You, then I believe You're going to give me peace and put me on the right path.

That's when I repented for the way I was acting and my strong desire to achieve and succeed at an earthly level. Even though I initially thanked God for getting to the major leagues, the reality is that I was playing for fame and recognition. I used to look in the mirror and be impressed. Imagine that. And now I was failing.

It's funny that it took so long for me to grasp this concept since I was playing a game where guys failed a lot every night. You only have to be successful three out of ten times at the plate to become a baseball superstar with a $100 million contract.

As I thought through my situation, I realized that when I kept my eyes focused on Christ instead of my problems, then I found freedom. But when I started struggling on the baseball field, I got off track because I turned the focus on myself. I did this for various reasons: excessive pride, lavish self-importance, and overblown conceit.

I was still a work in progress after spending a couple of days with Byron, but I did stop sharing every little depressing thought with Julianna. Instead, I focused on Philippians 4:6–7 (NIV): "Do not be anxious about anything, but in every situation, by prayer and petition, with thanksgiving, present your requests to God.

And the peace of God, which transcends all understanding, will guard your hearts and your minds in Christ Jesus."

I started to take my thoughts captive and make them obedient to Christ. Since I had Christ in my heart, whenever those dark thoughts came into my consciousness, I just reminded myself that I was a sinner saved by grace and God's power in my life was sufficient despite my weaknesses.

I put one foot in front of the other, regardless. I believed in faith despite my doubts. I prayed every day that God would bring me out of this funk, and if I still woke up feeling darkness and depression, then I resolved again to trust God and be faithful to what He had called me to do . . . being a solid husband for Julianna—someone she could count on—and working hard at my job.

Even though I steadied myself emotionally and felt like I turned a corner, I couldn't pull myself out of a downward spiral at the plate. In the midst of my hitting struggles, I tore the right oblique muscle—located on the side and front of the abdomen—in mid-August and was put on the DL (disabled list) for the rest of the season.

It was just as well. At the time, I was batting a woeful .155 in 31 games with the Devil Rays with just three extra-base hits in 97 plate appearances. With no pop to my bat and a one-walk-to-seven-strike-outs batting ratio, I really wondered if I was part of the team's plans for moving forward. All I could do was mentally regroup and concentrate on rehabbing my abdomen muscles.

Julianna and I had moved into a new place in south St. Petersburg, and I got into a routine where I would drive to a rehabilitation facility across town, do my rehab, and then come back.

I didn't even go to the Rays' games. The team said I could do my rehab in the morning and relax at my house the rest of the day with my wife.

We barely paid attention to what my teammates were doing. I'm afraid there wasn't much to cheer: although the Devil Rays didn't lose 100 games like the last season, our 66–96 win-loss record cemented our grip on the AL East cellar.

We watched a lot of *House Hunter* shows on HGTV and settled into a routine of monotony. We didn't have a place to move into back in Nashville when the season was over, so Julianna was saying we should look into buying our first place since we had a few bucks in the bank and shouldn't throw away money on rent.

I should have shown more interest, but I was indifferent to the whole home-buying process. When she said she wanted to fly to Nashville to do a "house hunting" trip, my attitude was *Fine. Whatever. If you think the house is good enough, then it's good enough.*

Julianna is such a strong person that she didn't say anything at the time. But one night, while we were laying in bed, I was whining again about being injured, not hitting major league pitching, and felt totally overwhelmed by life. I hugged her because I needed her close. "I need you right now," I said in a desperate, whiny voice.

Julianna pushed me away and sat up. "I NEED YOU!" she yelled.

Her response jolted me and shook me to the core. What she yelled awakened the man in me to stand up and stop putting the pressure on my wife. My life wasn't supposed to be all about me. It was supposed to be about *her*. I should be caring more about *her* welfare and bringing *her* closer to God instead of whimpering that the Lord didn't care about me anymore.

I needed to rein in my woe-is-me attitude and recognize that I needed to ask the Lord to forgive me for being so selfish and self-centered. Following this incident with Julianna, I did repent for my actions and for my attitude. I got on my knees and asked the Lord to forgive me for what I'd become—someone who doubted

Him, who feared for his own future, and was selfishly focused on himself.

I resolved to stop complaining to Julianna and strive to be positive and help her in any way I could. I became more attentive to our house search in Nashville, although I received my come-uppance at the closing when the escrow agent, a lady, purposely talked past me and spoke to Julianna directly about what needed to be done in finalizing the purchase of our first home. Everything was in Julianna's name—the loan docs, the house insurance, and the title work. I was considered the secondary owner. Although I was offended and Julianna was uncomfortable, I got what I deserved. *Dude, your house isn't even in your name.*

As for the other parts of my life, I felt like I turned a corner following the 2007 season. I started sleeping better. Four hours a night turned to five, then six hours a night without waking up. When I reached eight hours of blissful and replenishing sleep, I felt like a new man. In church, Pastor Byron's sermons hit a nerve, and I'd feel a tingle all the way through my body.

I felt like my whole body was coming to life again. I had energy and wanted to eat again. All the little things I took for granted before, even regularity in bodily functions, returned to normal. I was coming back to life as a person again, but this time not as a superhero but as a regular guy who had a beautiful, lovely wife that God had granted a responsibility to uphold in our marriage.

When ball clubs struggle, there's a saying: "Wait until next year."

In turns out that 2008 would be the year for major changes in our lives—me on the baseball field and Julianna with her singing.

14

SWING CHANGE

BEN

Julianna was thrilled to move into our first home, which turned out to be in Franklin, a city of 60,000 twenty miles south of Nashville. Franklin, founded in 1799, feels like a small town because of its historic brick-facade downtown dominated by a Civil War monument in the town square.

We wanted to put our own touches onto our new two-story, three-bedroom place, which meant ripping out old carpet, installing new flooring, purchasing new appliances, and repainting the interior walls. Our house renovations moved along smoothly, as did my rehabbing efforts.

As far as I was concerned, getting my body ready for the next baseball season was a full-time job, which meant applying myself to working out and getting stronger. My "office" was Showtime Sports Academy, an indoor 35,000-square-foot training facility filled with utility fields and nine batting cages with Iron Mike pitching machines.

One morning in December, I was taking cuts in the batting cage, alternating with Drew Sutton, a minor-league player who had played at Corpus Christi with me. We had become best friends, and Drew had been an usher at our wedding. He and I talked about the tough seasons we'd been through—me in the majors and Triple A and him at Double A.

We both looked up to see Showtime manager Tony Naile walking toward us. Accompanying him was a well-dressed guy a couple of years older than me. He wore a blue polo shirt, dark slacks, and loafers and looked liked he stepped off a country club golf course. His arms cradled a camera and a laptop computer.

"Ben, Drew, this is Jaime Cevallos. He's knocking on doors and wants to talk to players about hitting," Tony said.

My defenses shot up as I moved closer to the netting. I figured I was about to receive a different kind of pitch.

"Great to meet you guys," Cevallos said. "I'm a swing coach. I'd love to look at the mechanics of your swing and see if I can help both of you raise your average and hit for power. I believe my theories on hitting can change baseball."

My defensive posture turned into a healthy skepticism. I had been tutored on hitting by dozens of coaches through the years. As a professional ballplayer, I knew that hitting coaches or "swing gurus," especially the itinerant ones, were always trying to make their mark on guys like me so that they can tell others, *I helped so-and-so with his hitting.* I seriously doubted his hitting theories could change baseball.

"I appreciate you dropping by," I said. "Maybe some time we can get together. But if you'll excuse me . . ." I stepped back into the batter's box and resumed my batting practice with Iron Mike. I could tell Drew was dubious as well.

Even though we gave Cevallos the cold shoulder, he returned a few days later. This time, he made a different kind of delivery. "Just give me a few minutes," he said. "Let me video you guys and put something together. You come back the next day, and I'll give you the information I have. You can take it or leave it—no charge. You can either use the information, or if you don't think it's going to help, forget about it."

I shrugged my shoulders. What did we have to lose?

"Okay, we'll be here tomorrow," I said.

Little did I know that Jaime Cevallos was so determined to break into the "swing guru" business that he had trouble holding down a real job and was making ends meet with a $7 an hour job at a nearby golf course. Nor did I know that he had been studying the baseball swing since he played for Mount Saint Mary's University, where he transformed himself from a light-hitting shortstop with a .197 batting average to a .364 hitter his junior year. Nor was I aware that Cevallos believed that by changing certain positions within the swing, a hitter could make incredible improvements to his batting prowess.

Cevallos came and videoed Drew and me and then met with us the following day. I had seen video of my swing hundreds of times, but his computer program was set up in a way that I could compare my swing side-by-side with some of the good major league hitters at the time.

Cevallos made it clear that our swings were different than the swings of the top major league hitters. "You guys aren't getting into the power slot," he began, which directly led into his main theory about hitting: that my right arm (if I was batting right-handed) needed to be down and in closer to the body, which would get my bat parallel to the ground a lot sooner. Having my right arm locked into my side would allow me to tap into more power from my hips and my core. Do that, Cevallos said, and I would be adding a "power connection" to my swing.

I'm simplifying his theories about hitting, which differed considerably from the traditional advice to "swing down" onto the ball. Instead, Cevallos was talking about getting on the plane of the ball and driving through the pitch. "If you really want to drive the ball to all fields, you're going to have to get into this slot earlier in your swing and stay on that swing path throughout your swing," Cevallos explained. Then he gave us some helpful drills as well as MP30 Training Bats, which he had developed to teach hitters to take the wrists out of the swing and use the big muscles in the legs and hips to generate power.

I thanked Jaime for his time. Undertaking a swing change wasn't something any professional ballplayer blindly walks into. To be honest, changing the way I hacked at the ball involved a certain amount of risk. What if Cevallos' theories turned me into a *worse* hitter? If that happened, I'd be out of baseball. My .155 batting average in 2007 meant that I was swinging the bat like it was a wet newspaper. I was barely hanging on to the major leagues.

When I played in the minors, I was known as a "contact" hitter—someone who put the ball into play and hit a lot of singles. I was your typical "two-hole" batter—the No. 2 guy in the lineup who could advance the leadoff hitter if he got on base, execute the hit-and-run, or work the count for a walk so that I could get on base for the heart of our batting lineup—the 3, 4, and 5 hitters.

I also took a lot of pitches. I almost always lay off the first pitch, and if the first pitch was a ball, I took the second pitch. Even if I had a "hitter's count"—the 3-and-1 pitch—I usually left the bat on my shoulder. A walk is as good a hit, right?

When I reached the majors, though, I was facing much better pitching. Not only were the fastballs faster, but the precision of each pitch also took my breath away. It didn't take long for the scouting reports on me to circulate around the league. *Since Zobrist lays off the first pitch, burn a fastball down the middle and get ahead in the count.*

Major league pitchers would give me a fastball strike followed by a fastball to the corner that I would lay off, which left me in the hole facing an 0–2 count. That's when they turned nasty with hard-breaking curveballs or two-seam fastballs just off the plate. I had to protect myself, of course, which meant I had to swing. I usually put the ball weakly into play, resulting in an easy ground out or a force play.

I had to do something about my hitting, which was why I was open to listening to Jaime Cevallos. But I knew I had to get a second opinion before making any drastic changes in my batting style. We had planned a visit to Dallas to see Dan and Liz Heefner and their growing family, so it was good timing for some of the questions I had about Cevallos's theories. My brother-in-law, who, at that time, was the hitting coach at Dallas Baptist University, had always been smart about understanding the swing and helping his players figure out what makes their swings work.

Dan confirmed the stuff Jamie was saying about the right positions good hitters get into and getting on plane, and he added the idea of connecting everything together to create the most powerful type of swing. Dan liked talking about connection, while Jamie was all about positions and bat path.

Dan reminded me how I needed to get the lower half of my body moving in sync with my hands. He said that the hips and shoulders naturally want to separate from the hands when I was trying to put everything into motion at a very high speed, but if I could bring everything together, that would give me more power. Many batters are "handsy" with their swings instead of using the entire body when they receive the pitch.

"When you swing the bat, it's more than throwing the barrel of the bat at the ball," Dan said. "It's the strength of your legs, your hips, your shoulders, your arms, your hands, and the barrel all together, going into the baseball simultaneously."

That off-season, I worked diligently in the batting cage to incorporate Jaime's and Dan's concepts, making "mechanical" adjustments in the swing. I also decided that I had to be more aggressive at the plate, and that meant going after pitches earlier in the count. That included turning on the first pitch. Throughout the 2007 season, major league pitchers were giving me a hittable strike on the first pitch, which I let sail by. This time around, I would be hunting fastballs and swinging hard on them. I wasn't going to wait around and let the pitcher get ahead of me in the count and then dominate me with his nastiest stuff.

Since Jaime was local, Drew and I agreed to be his "experiment" during the off-season. "Okay, we'll go with this as long as we feel like it's helping our hitting," I said. "If it doesn't help, we'll forget about it and move along. But if we do improve, then we'll help you get your name out there."

Jaime continued to video us and show us where our bodies needed to be positioned during each phase of the swing. Seeing myself on video in this way was a revelation and burned a major impression in mind. When it came time to put Jaime's principles to work during spring training, I immediately saw good results. As I continued to hit the ball in spring training, my coaches were talking about keeping me around as a utility player. They saw me as someone who could play various positions in the infield and outfield.

I was determined that this year would be different. I would take more chances at the plate, and I would try new positions in the field. But more than anything, no matter what the results were,

I was going to be faithful to the simple daily things God called me to without whining. Of that, I was resolved.

JULIANNA

When spring training started, we rented a condo on 4th Street in St. Petersburg that was situated in what I would call a "transitional" neighborhood. There were million-dollar homes right next to low-income government housing.

One morning, we ran out of trash bags, so I decided to walk to a nearby CVS pharmacy and purchase some. I had my workout clothes on: a white tank top and tight black workout shorts. I put my hair up in a ponytail because it was so hot and sticky in Florida, even in March. I wore a small cross-body purse with my wallet and cell phone.

I walked a couple of blocks past a strip mall when I noticed two swarthy-looking guys in their twenties standing on the sidewalk ahead of me. They looked at me, and immediately my brain started processing what I saw. I was no longer the naïve girl who asked, "Dad, where are we going on vacation?" I was now extremely aware of my surroundings, and I wasn't getting a good vibe from these guys.

I immediately slowed and pulled out my cell phone. I knew Ben was on the field, so I called Drew Sutton, who was down in Florida but hadn't started spring training yet.

"Hey, Drew. It's Jules."

He must have heard the concern in my voice. "Are you okay?"

"I'm walking on 4th, and there are a couple of guys staring at me. I don't want to turn around because I don't want them to know where I live. Can you stay on the phone with me?"

"Of course."

I continued walking, holding the cell phone to my ear and looking down. I came upon the two men standing on the sidewalk, but they did not step out of the way to let me pass. Instead, I had to step off the sidewalk to get around them. I continued to chitchat with Drew to show them I was talking to somebody. When I was about a half-block past, they turned and started following me.

I had two more blocks to go until I arrived at CVS. I picked up my pace, but a furtive glance over my shoulder confirmed that they matched my speed. I started walking even faster, which they matched as well.

"Drew, they are coming after me."

"You run!"

I broke out into a sprint. Fright filled my chest and caused tears to stream down my face. Memories of an event that happened a long time ago flooded my consciousness. All I could think about was getting to the CVS store, where I could seek safety.

I maintained a lead as I stormed through the front door and rushed toward the back of the store. Perhaps I could hide somewhere . . . and that's when I saw a set of gray floppy doors marked "Employees Only."

I pushed my way into a stockroom filled with boxes of Bounty paper towels and other merchandise. A young female employee looked at me in shock. "What are you doing here?" she asked.

"Two guys are chasing me! I just ran two blocks, and I think they are coming in here to get me."

"I got your back! I'll watch for them. You wait in here."

I realized that Drew was still on the line. "Drew, I'm at CVS. I'm with a girl now. I'll call you later."

I sank down onto the floor, knees to my chest, head on my knees, just praying: "Oh, God, not again!"

Then I stood up and peeked through the door a little bit. I saw my new best friend standing in the aisle, eyes looking toward the front. Sure enough, the two guys walked in, looking for me.

As they worked their way through the store and moved closer, I became more and more afraid. I hid behind some boxes while my heart pounded. The longest five minutes of my life passed, and then the floppy doors sprung open.

"They're gone," my new best friend said.

I thanked her profusely and then called Drew to fill him in. I would have asked him to pick me up, but he was in the Orlando area.

I guess I would have to walk home. I waited for fifteen minutes before departing CVS, my eyes glued for the abductors' whereabouts. I hadn't walked half a block when I looked to my right toward a parking lot and spotted one of the guys sitting in the back of a beat-up truck. He jumped out and started chasing me. From across the street, the other guy sprang forth from some bushes and gave chase.

My heart rate shot up 1,000 percent. I turned and sprinted in the other direction as fast as my legs would take me. A Talbot's clothing store looked like safe harbor.

I ran inside, crying and sobbing with my hands on my knees.

A saleslady closed the distance. "What on earth happened to you?" she asked.

I fought to catch my breath. "Two guys are chasing me."

Just then, we looked toward Talbot's floor-to-ceiling glass windows and saw the two menacing men. They made eye contact, and walked slowly past the windows . . . staring.

"I'm calling the cops," the saleslady said. Even she was shaken by their looks.

A police cruiser arrived within minutes, and the policeman who listened to my story offered to give me a ride back to the apartment. Along the way, I told him that I was by myself because my husband was away at spring training.

"We can do something about that, ma'am," he said.

Calls were made, and for the rest of the afternoon, a police car was parked in the neighborhood and a cop walked the beat.

When Ben heard the story, he was very thankful that I was safe.

As for me, I was shook to the core. Once again, the incident dredged up bad memories from my past.

BEN

I was practicing while this was happening. When we finally talked on the phone, I could tell Julianna was upset by the incident. By the time I got home that late afternoon, she was feeling much better. In a way, I was thankful that Jules was very aware of her surroundings and cognizant of those guys. She did the right thing by running into the CVS store. She was a strong girl.

Toward the end of spring training, I faced my own adversity. During one exhibition game, I was leading off first base when I tried to steal second against a left-handed pitcher. It was called a "first move" play: when the pitcher came out of his stretch and started his pitching motion, I took off toward second base. Instead of throwing to the plate, the pitcher flung the ball to the first baseman, who whipped a throw to second base. I dove headfirst and tried to avoid the tag. As I slid past second base, I stuck out my left hand and jammed my thumb in the infield dirt.

I grimaced in pain. I had broken the tip of my thumb—almost in half.

Doctors told me that I would need four to six weeks to heal, but when my broken thumb didn't respond well to treatment, doctors had to go back in and stick a pin inside my thumb to keep the bone together. Consequently, I needed eight weeks to heal and didn't rejoin the Rays until the middle of May. (During the off-season, the team ownership simplified the name from "Devil Rays" to "Rays," which I was glad to see.)

I played a bit for two weeks and then was sent down to Durham. I hit the ball well in Triple A, which resulted in a promotion back to the parent club. As soon as I came back up, I hit a couple of home runs. That raised some eyebrows since I had never shown any power before, but I was sent down again.

I came back up a couple of weeks later, and got sent back down. Came up, got sent down again. Turns out I was the Rays' designated yo-yo guy for the 2008 season. It really wasn't anything against me; it's just the way things worked out for the team.

Eventually, I was brought up for good in August, which was fun because we were in a *pennant race.* There was a great vibe on the team since we were playing for a franchise that had never come close to a .500 record in its eleven-year history—and now we had a great chance to make the playoffs for the first time. The credit for changing the losing culture in Tampa started with new team ownership, general manager Andrew Friedman, and manager Joe Maddon, an outside-the-box thinker who likes to keep his team loose.

The reason I stuck with the club was that my swing changes were working. The proof was in the numbers. Forty-nine percent of my hits during the 2008 season were for extra bases (up from 20 percent in 2007 and 2006), which dramatically raised my slugging percentage (a measure of the power of a hitter) from .206 in 2007 to .505 in 2008.

I also lifted my batting average to a respectable .253 and hit 12 home runs in only 198 at-bats, good enough to lead all major-league middle infielders in at-bats per home run (one long ball for every 16.5 at-bats). It was tremendously exciting to hit four home runs during the final regular season series against the Detroit Tigers. I also showed my versatility by playing *six* positions: shortstop, second base, and third base and left field, center field, and right field.

We kept winning games, which excited baseball fans in the Tampa/St. Pete region and brought great energy to Tropicana Field. In September, we pulled ahead of our rivals, the New York Yankees and Boston Red Sox, and I finished on a tear. During the last week of the season in a must-win game, I hit a go-ahead single in a four-run eighth inning against the Detroit Tigers and followed that with a solo homer in the 11th inning to lift the Rays to an 8–7 win over the Tigers. I had seven RBIs that week, hitting .455 (10-for-22) and was named American League Co-Player of the Week. What I found amusing—since I'm of Swiss heritage—was that I received a luxury Swiss watch from Tourneau in recognition of my achievement.

We concluded the season in a strong manner, finishing two games ahead of the Red Sox with a 97–65 record, which surpassed the record for most wins by a team in a single season after finishing with the worst record the previous year.

After beating the Chicago White Sox in the American League Division Series, we won a classic Game 7 at home against the rival Boston Red Sox to win the American League pennant, setting off pandemonium as I charged the field to celebrate with my teammates. I really couldn't believe that I would get a chance to play in the World Series against the Philadelphia Phillies. Baseball's biggest stage had always meant a great deal to me.

The year 2008 was already shaping up to be something special. Not only had my revamped swing and new power made me viable in the major leagues, but we learned midway through the season that Julianna was expecting our first child.

JULIANNA

I was nearly six months along when the Rays made the World Series in late October. I was visibly pregnant, but that wasn't going to keep me from traveling to Philadelphia after we opened the seven-game series with a split of the two games in Tampa Bay.

It was cold in Philadelphia since we were in the last week of October. I'll never forget the team bus pulling up to our downtown hotel, where Philly fans weren't in the mood to show us any brotherly love. A few of them surrounded the bus, yelling crude things and flipping us the bird. That was Reminder No. 1 that the World Series was a big deal in Philadelphia.

Typically when I attend an away game, wives and families are seated in the same section, which makes the ballgame experience nice. You're surrounded by familiar faces and people you know. Not for this World Series. We were scattered around Citizens Bank Park, the Phillies' stadium.

I was smart enough not to wear a Rays jersey or ball cap to a World Series game, but one time I stood up while Ben was walking to the plate and yelled, "Go, Ben." That was enough for fans in our section to single me out.

One guy behind me yelled, "Your kid is going to be a @#$% moron!"

I couldn't let that one go, even though I had learned the hard way that you don't say anything to the fans because there's usually alcohol involved.

I uncomfortably turned around my pregnant body and made eye contact with the buffoon a few rows behind me. "Excuse me?" I said.

As expected, he yelled another rude comment that's not worth repeating. Other fans in our section egged him on. A few ketchup packages were thrown my way. At least it wasn't beer. Then he said, "Get the @#$% out of here."

I reached for my cell phone and called Security.

"Sorry, ma'am. There's nuthin' we can do," said a male voice.

Then I noticed another one of our players' wives get up and leave the section next door. Getting out of there was sounding like a better idea with every passing minute. I knew there was a "family room" that was made available to players' families after the game. We could go hang out there.

When I walked up to the concourse, I found a couple of players' wives who had the same idea—make a retreat to the family room. We were walking through the concourse, hearing more catcalls, when a guy in a Phillies cap nonchalantly walked past me and elbowed me in the stomach.

Another player's wife rushed to my defense. "Hey, what are you doing? You don't mess with her. Can't you see she's pregnant?"

I appreciated the way she gave the guy a piece of her mind as we made our way downstairs to the family room, where we commiserated about how horrible the hometown fans were. There wasn't much to cheer about since Philadelphia was winning.

After Game 3, nearly every wife or girlfriend of a Rays player flew back to Tampa because of the abuse. Only three of us stayed, including me. I guess I wanted to show the fans that I wasn't going to back down, but I also wanted to be there for Ben, who got a chance to start Game 1 and Game 4. I mean, this was the World Series. I knew enough baseball to understand that playing in the Fall Classic is often a once-in-a-lifetime experience for a ballplayer.

Unfortunately, Philadelphia would go on to win the World Series in five games, but 2008 turned out to be a year of transition for us. I was pregnant, which was a surprise since we weren't even trying, and Ben had made sweeping progress in his hitting and was super excited to be playing so well.

And I also recorded my first album.

MAKING HITS

BEN

Following the World Series, we received a wonderful check for $95,000 (after taxes), as part of my players' share. Talk about a windfall. "Let's use some of that money to get your songs professionally produced," I said to Julianna.

I hadn't forgotten the promise that I had made to Julianna's dad that I would support her music and her keen desire to write and sing her own music someday. Just as Jules had done so much to help me fulfill my dream of playing major league baseball, I felt like I should help her realize her singing ambitions as well.

Now that we had some money to pay for producing some of the songs that Julianna had started writing in Corpus Christi, I knew the timing was right. But we had to move quickly since my wife was six months pregnant at the time. Fortunately, she knew a lot of people in the music industry because of her work for Tiffany Lee as well as Krystal Meyers, an up-and-coming Christian rock singer. Julianna asked Mitch Dane, a twenty-year veteran who'd worked with artists like Jars of Clay and Bebo Norman, to go into the studio and help take her melodies and lyrics and transform them into songs.

JULIANNA

I'm not sure what was more fun about the creative process: producing my songs into music on a CD or doing the photo shoot for the album cover and inside pages because I love dressing up.

During December 2008 and early January 2009, we produced seven songs for an extended play CD called *The Tree*. All in all, it probably took a good week to make the songs and sounds I wanted as well as lay down the vocal tracks.

If you've never listened to my music, it's hard to categorize. Sure, there are some pop elements, but I like layering in synthesized techno sounds and giving my songs a club-mix sound. My songs don't sound like the "praise and worship" music sung every Sunday morning in churches around the country.

My taste in music has always been eclectic. I grew up listening to Michael Jackson and Gloria Estefan and mainstream artists who could make me dance like the Ting Tings. I love the avant-garde sounds of Lady Gaga and the raw blues rock of the Black Keys. When I drive around town, I like to listen to P!nk, Radiohead, and a French electro house artist known as Madeon through my iPhone for my music fix. I'm vitally interested in what's happening in all genres of pop music, which come in many forms.

We had to be creative for my photo shoot since, in January, I was in my eighth month of pregnancy. This meant all head shots from different angles and different hairstyles and lighting. For someone who loves fashion and dressing up, posing before the camera was like catnip.

BEN

I got a kick out of the whole process. Writing songs, making an album, doing a photo shoot—all these things were something that Julianna had wanted to do since she was a little girl. She even decided on what music should be playing in the background while they were shooting under the lighting boxes.

On January 19, 2009, twelve days before the birth of Zion, we hosted a CD release party at 3rd & Lindsley, a music venue/restaurant in downtown Nashville. Nothing was going to stop her: Julianna had her band behind her, and from the moment her drummer counted off "one-two-three-four," Julianna sang and performed like she usually does—all out. The way she jumped around on stage and worked the microphone, I thought, *She's going to pop right here if she keeps moving like that.*

I'd say more than three hundred friends and music industry acquaintances were there that night, including two people who wouldn't miss this evening for anything—her parents.

JULIANNA

I knew Mom and Dad were happy that all the hard work they put into me—over twenty years—had come to fruition. I know they were proud of helping me develop my musical talent. And though no words were said, I felt like my parents were aware that Ben had kept his promise. The whole idea behind making a record was that this was going to be the culmination of my education. If I did nothing else with music, I could always say that I went through the process of writing and recording my own songs. Doing the photo shoot. Handing Mom and Dad a copy of *The Tree* CD. All in all, a very rewarding experience.

Mom returned a week or so later to help with my first delivery, but the night before Zion's birth, she got news that her father died of cancer in Louisiana. We made arrangements for Mom to fly to Baton Rouge to be with her family on the morning of February 1, 2009, the same time contractions started. She was already in the air when Ben rushed me to the maternity ward at 11:30 a.m. I wouldn't say the delivery process was easy, but it was quick. A few hours later, Zion Benjamin Zobrist entered the world. We liked the name Zion because of the alliterative "z" sound with our last name but more because Zion means "dwelling place for God."

Following the funeral in Louisiana, Mom flew back to Nashville to help me out before returning home to Iowa City. Ten days later, we had to leave for spring training, but we took the circular route. First, we drove to Dallas to see Dan and Liz and their three children. Everyone got to see Zion, and plenty of copies of my CD were handed out. Then we stopped in Louisiana to see Grannie Annie and console her after she lost her lifelong partner. It was a great joy to hand her a personal copy of my new CD.

BEN

Even though I finished strong in 2008 and had started two World Series games, I didn't know how much I would play after Opening Day. That was out of my control. What I could control was my choice of walk-up music. Sometimes called "entrance music," walk-up music is a snippet of a song that's played loudly over the stadium speakers whenever a hometown hitter walks from the on-deck circle to home plate. During the '08 season, I strode to the plate with "Ignition" from Christian artist TobyMac firing me up.

There was no question in my mind that I was going to use one of Julianna's songs as my walk-up song in 2009. Her songs were all somewhat rock tunes, but the larger point is that I wanted fans to know that Julianna was part of my team every time I stepped into the batter's box. I wasn't out there by myself. Julianna was part of what I was doing on the field.

I chose "The Tree," the single, because that was my favorite song on her CD. I liked the piano in the song as well as the depth of the lyrics. It's the gospel. To me, that was the song I wanted to play.

It didn't take too long for one of the beat writers, Marc Topkin of the *Tampa Bay Times*, to pick up on my choice of walk-up music.

"Your walk-up song . . . who's singing that?" he asked one time in the locker room.

"That's my wife, Julianna. She's a musician."

"She's pretty good," Topkin allowed.

When you hear professional athletes say, "My wife sings," that can mean anything. But Julianna was a pro. She had studied music and been part of the industry before our marriage. She knew how the music world worked and what she was doing behind a microphone stand. She could flat-out sing.

Topkin wrote a feature story about Julianna and how I had chosen one of her songs off her debut CD to be my walk-up music. Someone in the Rays' front office must have seen the story because it wasn't too long afterward that we received a request: Would Julianna like to sing the National Anthem before one of our home games?

I stood on the dugout steps, hat off, beaming as Julianna took the microphone and stood near home plate to belt out our National Anthem before the start of our interleague game against the Philadelphia Phillies. This was a rematch, if you will, of two World Series teams.

The date was June 25, 2009, the 74th game of the season and nearly the half-way point. My swing changes were working with big increases in average and power: I was batting .289 with 15 home runs and an on-base percentage of .399.

In the bottom of the first, batting fifth, I homered to left field. It wasn't quite Babe Ruth promising the sick kid in the hospital bed that he'd hit one out, but it sure was a lot of fun to round the bases just fifteen minutes after my wife sang the National Anthem.

The 2009 season turned out to be my break-out year, even though I wasn't a starter when the season opened. I probably played twice a week the first month of the season, but when I got in there, I ripped doubles and home runs. Then I had some pinch-hit home runs to tie games in May, which managers always love.

The hitting changes I had made with Jaime Cevallos and my brother-in-law Dan Heefner had turned me into a different batter. When pitchers started me out with fastballs, I no longer let their first offerings fly by. I swung aggressively with my new power stroke. I had transformed myself from a work-the-count, slap-the-ball-to-all-fields hitter to someone who was a threat to go deep.

When our second baseman, Akinori Iwamura of Japan, tore up his knee trying to turn a double play in mid-May, I got a chance to take the field every day. I kept playing at a high level—and didn't take my foot off the gas. The doubles and home runs kept coming off my bat. A week before the All-Star break, my manager, Joe Maddon—who had taken to calling me "Zorilla" to the media—surprised a few folks when he selected me to the All-Star team. "There's a form of nepotism involved, but you don't want to be anti-nepotist, if that's a word. I just felt his numbers stacked up real well," Joe told reporters.

Not only had I hit an attention-getting 17 home runs the first half of the season, but I led the American League in on-base slugging percentage (OPS) with 1.015.

The fact that the 80th All-Star game was being held in St. Louis—where just seven years earlier I had snuck down behind home plate to check out the velocity of major league pitching, much like a kid pressing his cheeks against the window display at a toy store—was an irony that I couldn't overlook. Of course Julianna and my parents and other family members were there after I scrounged up every spare ticket I could find. I struck out in my only at-bat, but I had already died and gone to baseball heaven when I was introduced before the game with the illustrious All-Stars from both leagues.

I continued tattooing the ball in the second half of the season. The Rays had another really good year, finishing 84-78, but we missed landing a wild-card playoff berth because the New York Yankees and Boston Red Sox had bigger years.

When the final game was in the books, my power improvement at the plate was there for everyone to see in black-and-white: I batted .297 in 152 games and hit 27 home runs, 28 doubles, and 7 triples. All those extra-base hits gave me a career-high slugging average of .543, good for seventh in the league. And even though I tailed off in the second half with my on-base slugging percentage, my mark of .948 was still fourth best in the league. I was also fourth best in on-base percentage (.405).

What the seamheads—those who study the minutiae of baseball statistics in a discipline known as sabermetrics—loved was my WAR, or wins above replacement. The WAR estimates the number of wins that a player provides over a "replacement" player from the minor leagues or the bench by taking into account the player's offense, defense, and base-running statistics. The WAR does not reflect your pure talent, but it is a useful indicator of how valuable you are to the team.

I led the American League in WAR with 8.6, was second in Above Replacement, third in Offensive WAR, and fourth in defensive WAR, which meant I did good glove work. There were a lot of other esoteric categories—Adjusted OPS, Adjusted Batting Runs, and Adjusted Batting Wins—where I was among the top three.

The Tampa Bay organization was suddenly interested in keeping me around. They believed I was going to be a productive major league player for years to come, so they began negotiating with my agent before the 2010 season. What the Rays did was basically offer to buy out my three arbitration seasons and my first two years of free agent eligibility.

During the negotiations, it came down to the proverbial bird-in-the-hand versus two-in-the-bush: the security of a five-year deal versus going year-to-year and being able to negotiate a much higher contract if my game continued at the same high level.

In the end, I chose security as well as a strong desire to stay in Tampa Bay, where I loved playing for Joe Maddon and the Rays organization. My contract, which contained two option years for 2014 and 2015, meant a pay raise from $453,000 to roughly ten times that amount and would mean more ($7 million a year in 2014 and $7.5 million a year in 2015) if Tampa Bay chose to exercise my option years.

Of course, these are all fantastic amounts of money, and Julianna and I seek to be good stewards of the resources that God has provided. I realize how fortunate I am to have an organization that really believes in me as a player and a manager who has my back like Joe Maddon. A lot of my success can be traced to Joe's decision to give me grace when I got sent back down and back up and back down and back up in 2008. Not many coaches would have stuck with a player like that, but he gave me a chance to show how I could play this great game.

I think I've held up my part of the bargain. I've been a solid player since the 2010 season. The Rays have generally used me at second base and right field, which has allowed the team valuable roster flexibility. I played a lot of shortstop during the 2012 season and loved making the throws from deep in the hole once again.

In 2013, Joe moved me back and forth between right field and second base as the situation warranted it, and I was very pleased with how the season played out. I was shocked to be picked to the American League All-Star roster as the Rays' lone representative. Other guys on our club were having great years, like our home-run hitting third baseman Evan Longoria and left-handed pitcher David Price, but the American League manager, Detroit's Jim Leyland, said he picked me because I could play anywhere and I was a switch-hitter.

After the All-Star break, we returned to the playoffs after winning a thrilling wild-card playoff game against the Cleveland Indians only to run into our nemesis, the Boston Red Sox. After falling behind 2–0 in the best-of-five series, we hosted the Red Sox at home. Julianna sung the National Anthem, which she says is the hardest but also her favorite song to sing. She did a great job. I gave her a congratulatory hug moments after she hit the difficult notes to "O'er the land of the free and the home of the brave."

Jules outdid herself when she sang "God Bless America" during the seventh-inning stretch, which was carried live nationally on TBS. I stood on the first step of the dugout and beamed. Then I advanced to the on-deck circle, and batting second in the inning, I knocked a pitch into left field for a single. That was a thrill, as was Jose Labaton's walk-off home run in the bottom of the ninth to claim a clutch come-from-behind, win-or-go-home playoff game. Unfortunately, we were eliminated from the playoffs the next night by the Red Sox, who went on to win the 2013 World Series in front of their fans at Fenway Park.

On the personal side for 2013, I felt like I had a solid year with a .275 batting average, a .354 on-base percentage, and 12 home runs. I was very pleased when the Tampa Bay organization exercised its option and picked me up for the 2014 season.

Some day, I'd like to show Joe and the Rays' fans how versatile I can really be. I'd love to play all nine positions in a nine-inning game. It's been done four times in major league history; the most recent being Shane Halter for the Detroit Tigers in 2000.

Catching would be tough, but the pitching part doesn't scare me. I've already told Joe that if we're in the sixteenth inning and have run out of arms, I'm his man. I would really like to try my hand at pitching because I was on the mound a lot at Olivet Nazarene.

Maybe Joe will turn me loose some time.

We'll just have to wait and see.

A NEW LINEUP
CARD

BEN

Following my breakout season with the Rays in 2009, the publicity from playing well suddenly gave me a "platform"—an opportunity to touch people's lives and share what was important to me either through the media or through speaking events and personal appearances. Overnight, it seemed like I received dozens of requests to speak in school classrooms, sports banquets, fundraising events, and evangelical outreaches. I said yes to as many invitations as I could because I *love* talking about what really matters in life and sharing God's love with audiences.

Then something interesting happened after Julianna put out her first CD and people heard for themselves that she was an accomplished singer and songwriter. The resulting publicity in the Tampa area allowed locals to begin to know us as a couple. It's not every day that a professional baseball player had a Christian singer as his wife, so that notoriety led to requests—mainly from local churches—for me to speak and for Julianna to sing.

We had to pick and choose what we said yes to because Julianna had an infant boy who needed her around-the-clock during the 2009 season. But the times that Julianna and I would appear together were a lot of fun, especially because this was something that we could do together. Even though Julianna's budding music career was a part-time effort, she was fine with that. She knew she didn't have the luxury of devoting herself 100 percent to her music, especially after our second child, Kruse Allegra Zobrist, came along on September 19, 2011.

But choosing to invest in our marriage and raise Zion and Kruse—often as a single mom since I'm on the road half the season—showed where her heart lay. It was an honorable thing for her to put family first because, if she wanted to, Julianna could have arranged full-time nannies and poured her energies into trying to make it in the music world—touring, doing interviews, making appearances, and showing up at media events. But that would mean time away from the kids and me, and she wasn't willing to do that.

That's one reason why I love Julianna so much, but I always wanted her to make the most out of her singing and songwriting ability while I sought to maximize my God-given talent on the baseball diamond. When Zion turned four and Kruse hit the toddler years in 2013, we felt we could say yes more often to the requests from churches to hear me speak and Julianna sing.

During the 2013 season, we came up with an event where we would share our story in between seven or eight songs sung by Julianna. The goal was to be transparent and discuss our hard times while encouraging others in their personal troubles and pointing them to Christ.

If a church or community organization within a one-hour radius of Tampa invited us and could work with our schedule, we said yes. We could only do these evening events on my day off during the week or on nights after a day ball game, which were Sundays or the occasional weekday, and we really enjoyed ourselves.

JULIANNA

I loved how Ben wanted to support my music as much as I supported his baseball. Doing shows together turned out to be something special, so let me describe what a typical show looks like.

While Ben is playing his day game at Tropicana Field, I'll drive with Zion and Kruse to the church or venue, usually arriving around 3 o'clock in the afternoon. Or I'll have my assistant—usually a young woman who gives me a hand with the kids—drive Zion and Kruse after they wake up from their afternoon naps.

Whether or not my kids are with me, my band and their equipment usually follow in a van. I have four local guys who play behind me whenever I sing in the Tampa Bay area: a guitar player, a bass player, a keyboardist, and a drummer. When I travel to a gig outside of Florida—like the time I sang at Angelus Temple in Los Angeles during the 2013 season—I bring along a DJ who plays tracks behind me as well as a synthesizer to perform a fun, upbeat show.

My band's load-in takes around forty-five minutes. While they're setting up their equipment and doing a line check, I retreat to the green room—a waiting room behind the stage that is never painted green, I might add. If the kids are with me, either my assistant or someone with the church will take them for a spell while I run through twenty to twenty-five minutes of vocal exercises. I begin by putting on headphones and listening to a set of scales that my vocal instructor put together. Then I sing along to the various notes to get my voice warmed up.

Once the band's line check is done, I receive a text from my guitar player, John B., that says, *Jules, ready 4U.*

With my vocal cords loosened up, I'll walk out to the stage for a mic check. I also have flesh-colored audio monitors in my ears and a wireless pack attached to my skirt on my back.

We basically run through a couple of the songs we'll be performing that night. My band also wears in-ear monitors, so they'll shoot a thumb's up or thumb's down to the soundboard guy to either raise or lower the sound of my voice in their ears. The lighting person also adjusts the lights while we're working out the sound mix.

Sometime during the sound check, I'll walk out into the middle of the seating area, with the band still playing and me still singing, so that I can listen to how the sound is turning out. It's amazing how much work it takes to get things right.

When we're done, it's back to the green room, where I hang out with the kids before the show. Ben shows up around dinner time, having driven straight from the stadium to the venue. They usually have some sort of chicken or pasta dinner prepared for us, which is fine. I'm not a greasy food or sweets type of girl before I perform.

One of my favorite things before the show happens when the pastor or youth pastor drops by to say hello and pray for us. We gather in a circle and take turns praying that God would be part of the evening, that He would be glorified, and that the gospel would be made clear.

BEN

Churches often use our appearances as outreach events to attract people in the community who haven't darkened a church door in ages. It's always my prayer that people won't exalt us, but they would exalt God during the event. We want God to open up their hearts and see what God has done through us, not anything we have done.

We often start the show with a video montage of some of my more climatic moments on the baseball field: being part of the 2008 World Series team; slapping singles, doubles, and home runs; turning a double play; or throwing out a runner from right field when he tried to tag up on a sacrifice fly.

When we appear in the Tampa-St. Pete area, it's not uncommon for dozens to show up in white Tampa Bay jerseys with navy piping or navy ball caps with the TB logo. That's why the MC for the evening usually starts by shouting, "Are there any Rays fans in the house?"

I hear the whoops and hollers from the side of the stage, and they're even louder if we won that day or are having a good run.

Then the MC says some nice things about us and reminds everyone that if they've seen me bat at Tropicana Field, then they've heard Julianna sing as part of my walk-up music. And then we're introduced.

I usually try to play off the energy of the fans. After thanking everyone for coming out, I'll say, "We got a good win today against the Yankees," or if I struggled and struck out a couple of times in a losing effort, I'll fall back on that baseball cliché that we'll get them next time.

But I don't gab for long because the band is sounding the first notes to Julianna's opening song, "Heartbeat."

JULIANNA

"Heartbeat" is one of the songs on my new CD that's releasing in 2014. The song has an epic dubstep-driven chorus:

We're raising hope
We come alive
Clear the wreckage long enough
To see the light
We're raising hope
Parting skies
Hand in hand
One heartbeat at a time
One heartbeat at a time

It took me the 2013 season to write all the songs on this new album. If I wasn't on the road with Ben, I would fly back to Nashville with the kids and work until we met back in Tampa or another city. I loved working with great producers like Chuck Butler and Seth Jones on the various tracks.

When we finish "Heartbeat," Ben returns from the wings and we start sharing our story—beginning with how we met and how Ben turned a $50 tryout into a college baseball experience. We share many of the same stories we've told you about in *Double Play*, and we're just as real in person as we are on the printed page. What makes our presentation unique, I think, is how we intersperse our story with several more of my songs:

- "Crazy Fearless" comes after we talk about our Corpus Christi days and getting traded from the Astros organization to the Tampa Bay Rays.
- "Behind Me" comes after Ben got called up and how he handled the newfound attention from playing in the major leagues, which meant he had to deal with pride and the pressure to be everything to everybody.
- "Only You" comes after Ben's bout with depression during the 2007 season, and I also share my reaction to his struggles.

- "Common Ground" comes after we describe what
  we've learned about life, which is that there is great
  depth to our own depravity that surfaces when we
  come to the end of ourselves and learn to depend on
  Christ. The point we emphasize is regardless of one's
  circumstances, no one is exempt from life's struggles.
  We tell people that the gospel puts everyone on common ground. We are all sinners before a Holy God. No
  one person is greater than another. We all needed Jesus
  to die on a cross for our sins.

We usually do a couple more songs and finish with "Say It
Now" off my second CD, a high energy, up-tempo song that gets
people clapping. When we're done with the seventy-five minute
show, we'll do a question-and-answer time, which is always interesting because you never know what folks are going to ask.

"Say It Now," the title track of my second CD, slowly gained
the attention of the music industry. Some fun opportunities came
along, such as when another song on the CD, "Behind Me," was
selected to be the "single of the week" for iTunes in July 2012. I
thought it was terrific that iTunes embraced the song. The song
was also selected as a special value-added single for Lifeway's
Positively Hits campaign.

BEN

I like how Julianna's songs match up with where we are in our
story. When our program is over, we invite people to drop by our
table in the back for autographs and pictures.

It's very gratifying to meet people who made the effort to come
see us. They often thank us for sharing our struggles and mention
that they've had their hard times as well. I'm especially humbled

when parents tell me that I've been a good role model for their son and how they're happy to point to a guy who's a Christian and willing to share his faith and walk with Christ in a public way.

JULIANNA

Ben and I sit behind a six-foot table where I sign CDs purchased from the merchandise table. Ben has a stack of his testimony cards that he signs, but lots of times people come through wanting him to attach his autograph to a Rays jersey or a Tampa Bay ball cap. And we're happy to pose for pictures.

Usually when I'm talking to young girls, it's not uncommon for the conversation to begin with fashion or style, which is fine with me since fashion is another one of my interests. Regardless of where the conversation goes, I love getting to meet and talk with young women. They are fascinating and smart, and I remember like it was yesterday being their age with so many dreams and goals lying ahead. I encourage everyone to become our friend on Facebook or follow us on Twitter or Instagram to stay connected.

One time, after finishing a performance, a woman close to my age pulled me aside and said, "I wish I could do what you do, but I'm just a mom!"

"You don't have to feel that way," I replied. "God still wants you to follow your passion, whatever that may be. If you really enjoy painting or something like that, you don't have to put it aside just because you think it's more godly to focus on your children 24/7. Go ahead and take an hour of your day to paint or whatever it is that you like to do and brings you happiness. It would also be good for your children to see you exercising the talents God has given you."

It's all in striking the right balance. If I can reach young women and girls with the message that they don't have to put pressure on themselves to be perfect, doing so means a great deal to me. I like showing others that Christian pop or Christian alternative music—or whatever musical category folks plug me into—can be fun and infectious and just as good as anything the world has to offer.

I love touching people's hearts with my music because songs stir the soul and lift one's spirits. I'm grateful that singing was something God planted in my heart as a young girl.

BEN

Julianna and I are just trying to be faithful with the circumstances and opportunities that God puts in our lives on a daily basis. When it comes to opportunities to speak and sing, we want to be faithful to what God is giving us to do. Sure, I'd love to play golf on my day off or just hang around the pool watching the kids get wet, but as long as our shows don't encroach on our main priorities of glorifying God in our relationship with each other and with our kids, we're willing to say yes because we just want to be faithful with the platform He's given us for this short time.

FINAL OUT

JULIANNA

There's a major reason why I've had to be patient and not commit as much time as I would like to writing and recording songs, as well as performing them, and it's because of Ben's demanding travel schedule with baseball.

Right after Ben and I got married, we had an important conversation about what our married life would look like, and we both agreed that if Ben was going to do baseball, then we needed to commit to being together. We heard that the divorce rate among baseball couples was very high—around 84 percent, which is considerably higher than the national divorce rate, where one out of every two marriages fail.

If we didn't want to become another marital casualty, then we had to be proactive. So we did something about it. We decided that we would never be apart for longer than six days.

That's why, even in the minor leagues when money was tight, Ben and I committed to having me drive or fly to cities where Ben was playing, like the time in Indianapolis when Ben lost it outside the natural history museum. In the major leagues, road trips usually last eight to twelve days, sometimes longer, which makes for some creative traveling itineraries, especially now that we have children.

Depending on the length of Ben's road trip and the cities he's going to, I'll meet him at the beginning, middle, or end. There have been occasions when Ben will play a Sunday afternoon game in Tampa and fly to Boston after the game to start a three-series swing through Boston, New York, and Baltimore, but I leave with the kids that morning to meet Ben in one of those three cities that evening. I usually like to go to Boston during those Northeast swings because the team hotel is in the middle of downtown, near parks and within walking distance of Fenway Park. When I go to New York, the team stays right in the middle of Times Square, a fifteen-minute stroll from Central Park.

The kids and I are allowed to stay with Ben at the team hotel. Since our children are involved, my trips involve lots of forethought and organizing with the Rays' travel secretary because if I check into the hotel before the team arrives, I have to be on the reservation or the front desk will not let me into the room until Ben arrives.

As any young mother will attest, it's not easy doing the plane, trains, and automobile thing with a preschooler and a toddler. Zion, to his credit, has become a travel pro and my little assistant. You should see us after we park the car at the Tampa International Airport. I push Kruse in her stroller with one hand while pulling a rolling luggage with other and balancing a purse and travel bag around my neck. Zion wears his travel backpack and rolls a small suitcase behind him. After dragging our bags to check-in, he helps me through security. Zion has the routine down and automatically takes off his shoes and places his backpack and luggage through the metal detector. He also helps push my stuff through.

Flights usually last two or three hours. Upon arrival, we gather our luggage and head to the hotel. Once we're settled, it's a challenge to keep the kids entertained when it's just you and the four walls. That's why I prefer cities with lots of parks nearby.

I go through all this trouble and endure plenty of travel headaches for our marriage. It would be very easy for me to start my own life, have my own music career, and raise the kids by myself; we do our thing and Ben does his thing. I could stay in Nashville, and Ben would have an apartment in Tampa Bay. Sure, we would be together in the offseason and see each other in the summer, but ours would be a long-distance relationship. That would be the easy choice and what many baseball families do, but we wanted to do what was right for our family. We chose a different route because we don't want a typical "baseball marriage."

Our no-longer-than-six-days-apart policy means lots of travel and many sacrifices on my part, but it's also a sacrifice for Ben. When we're all together in Boston, New York, Chicago, or any other American League city, he doesn't get to sleep in or relax the rest of the morning and early afternoon until he has to go to the ballpark. (Ballplayers rarely get to bed before 1:00 a.m. after a night game.) I have the kids on a midnight-to-10:00 a.m. schedule, but even then, the kids will sometimes get up earlier because of the time change or new surroundings, which mean Ben can't sleep anymore. Usually, we go out for breakfast or brunch, which is nice but not always relaxing.

Every parent knows that raising children involves more than ordering room service or taking them out to eat. Child-rearing takes a lot of mental power when you're trying to parent the right way. That can be draining on Ben on game days, but we both know that we made our travel policy so that our marriage, and parenting, can stay strong.

For those of you wondering what will happen when Zion reaches school age, we'll just have to see where we are in a couple of years.

Fortunately, I know something about homeschooling.

BEN

I can't praise Julianna enough for what she does to keep the family together. While traveling to some of the nation's biggest cities sounds glamorous, trudging through airports, dealing with security checkpoints, hailing taxis, checking into hotels, and finding restaurants to feed hungry kids gets old quickly. Their lives would be simpler if they didn't come out on the road with me, but that's the investment we're willing to make for our marriage.

When I'm alone on the road, however, I like to spend time digging into God's Word and reading good books such as:

- *What Every Son Wishes His Father Had Told Him* by Byron Forrest Yawn, my pastor at Community Bible Church in Nashville
- *Five English Reformers* by J. C. Ryle (biographies of English martyrs burned at the stake during Queen Mary's reign in the sixteenth century)
- *Church History in Plain Language* by Bruce Shelley (a fascinating examination of the decline in traditional mainline denominations)
- *Attributes of God* by Arthur W. Pink (a discussion of seventeen attributes of God, including His sovereignty, patience, love, and faithfulness)

As you can tell, theology is something I've always been interested in. These books have helped me reflect on my relationship with God and how the Lord is using my life to bring more attention to what He is doing. I want people to realize that our stories are just smaller narratives in God's much-greater story.

I've thought a great deal about the story my Lord and Savior, Jesus Christ, is writing right now for me. I know that making the majors in two-and-a-half years after getting drafted in the sixth round doesn't happen very often. When I got called up, I'll never forget the joy I felt running onto a major-league field for the first time after the National Anthem had been sung.

This is un-be-lieve-able. Look at this stadium! I'm playing against the best players in the world. This is incredible, God. Help me to use it for Your glory.

Today, I'm no longer impressed with myself because I saw the hole in my heart while I chased success. The reality is that success will never satisfy you, not even if you become a .300 hitter, make the All-Star team, or sign a huge multi-year, multi-million-dollar contract. There will always be the next big thing.

Fortunately, I have Julianna by my side to keep me grounded. She has been absolutely amazing throughout this entire process, and I thank the Lord for the opportunities He's given both of us in baseball and music—a "double play," if you will.

The baseball term *double play* is an apt metaphor for our situation. When I think about a double play as a ballplayer, the goal is to get two outs in one play. Not only do double plays expedite the game, but if your team is in a jam, a double play gets you out of the inning quickly.

What baseball fans don't see is the sacrifice that has to be made before the double play ever happens. When you're playing for two outs, the entire infield has to give up ground. All four infielders take a few steps in toward the plate and play outside of their normal position. You're trusting that the sacrifice you're making is going to pay off in the end.

Julianna has had to make sacrifices to enable us to stay together as a family, such as the long-distance trips she makes with the kids so that we're never apart for longer than six days. She's also had to make her music career a part-time venture because of my profession and her desire to be a mom. She's made those choices to serve me and to serve Christ.

We know that we lead unconventional lives, just as there are unconventional double plays. Life sometimes isn't a 6-4-3 or 4-6-3 double play, as they go down in the scorebook. The more unusual double plays take creativity and forethought, which means ballplayers have to know *exactly* what they'll do when the ball is hit in their direction. For infielders, a line drive means while one infielder is reacting toward the ball, the other infielder is covering a base to double up a runner. There can be no hesitation, or the double play will never happen.

Double plays in baseball—whether fantastic or boring—are difficult. There's no perfect way to get the job done, but it takes skill and preparation to turn two. You have to be willing to be flexible, go where the ball bounces, and make the play that works.

People often ask me how I play multiple positions and why I don't demand to play one position. My answer is that I should do what's best for the team. Sacrificing my comfort as a player is a small example of what every follower of Christ is called to do in our walk with Him.

On the ball field, this mind-set has enabled me to be a team player. When I'm open to God's leading in all areas of life, it's amazing to watch what He can do. He transformed my heart from an egotistical, self-centered, know-it-all to someone who's ready to be used in a way that gives the team the best chance to win.

I'm incredibly thankful to the Lord that Julianna and I have been able to share our story. Like every married couple, we've made errors and failed to cover bases, but we've done our best to dust ourselves off and be ready for whatever play comes next. What pleases me a great deal is how my baseball and her singing make us a unique double-play combination, but that's really an example of God's creativity, not ours.

Julianna and I are excited about what the future holds. I hope the miraculous way we were introduced to each other and the things we've learned along the way have inspired and encouraged you. I can assure you that our confidence is in Christ, and our peace and satisfaction come from Him.

So we hope to see you the next time the umpire yells, "Play ball!"—or when Julianna's band strikes up the first chords.

Maybe you'll see a double play.

INVITE BEN AND JULIANNA ZOBRIST TO SPEAK AND SING AT YOUR EVENT

Ben and Julianna Zobrist are a dynamic husband-and-wife team who love to encourage others to live life with thoughtful and self-less intention.

If you would like to invite them to your next event, please contact:

Jay Schield

Over the Line

615-668-5500

schieldj@bellsouth.net

The Zobrists' website, www.thezobrists.com, includes a link where people can find out more information on how to bring Ben and Julianna to your hometown or church.